MODELLING
Armoured Cars of World War II

MODELLING
Armoured Cars of World War II

Robin Buckland

THE CROWOOD PRESS

First published in 2021 by
The Crowood Press Ltd
Ramsbury, Marlborough
Wiltshire SN8 2HR

enquiries@crowood.com

www.crowood.com

British Library Cataloguing-in-Publication Data
A catalogue record for this book is available from the British Library.

ISBN 978 1 78500 906 8

Typeset by Simon and Sons
Cover design by Blue Sunflower Creative
Printed and bound in India by Parksons Graphics Pvt. Ltd., Mumbai.

Contents

Dedication

I need to thank the magazine editors I wrote for over many years, especially Ray Rimmell for starting me off with my Armoured Column in *Airfix* magazine back in 1985, and then both Ken Jones and Kelvin Barber for their support in writing my Small Scale Scene column in *Military Modelling* magazine for over thirty years. Ken also put his trust in me to look after the MilitaryModelling.com website, which I did from 2009 to the end of 2017. Thanks must also go to those manufacturers who supported me with information and samples over all those years, as I couldn't have done it without your support. I'd also like to thank fellow MAFVA member Vincent Mifsud for his assistance with the 3D printing project. There are too many others to mention them all, but in particular I'd like to remember my great personal friend, Barry Walby of MMS Models, who sadly passed away at the end of February 2020.

Most important of all, however, I'd like to dedicate this book to my lovely wife Una, who has had the amazing tolerance to put up with me and my modelling obsession, a hobby that has kept me occupied for well over fifty years.

Introduction

Many years ago now, I was motivated into getting into the hobby of modelling military vehicles thanks largely to the articles in *Airfix* magazine, way back in the 1960s. They also did a series of small hardback modelling guides, tackling a varied mix of topics and covering vehicles, aircraft, warships and figures. One of them was *Modelling Armoured Cars*, by Gerald Scarborough. In those days there were relatively few model kits available on the market, and many needed to be scratch-built. Now, around fifty years later, the variety of models on the market, in a multitude of scales, make modelling a very different ball game.

My main aim in this new book is to encourage modellers, and maybe wargamers as well, to explore the topic more widely. There is a whole range of military vehicles out there that are that bit different to the glamourous tank, which so often gets the limelight. I don't intend this to be an encyclopaedia of every armoured car, or indeed every kit in every scale. To attempt to do so would I think be doomed, as new kits are appearing all the time, plus I am sure there are some I haven't come across up to now. The aim is rather to look at just how broad the subject is, and give an idea of the wide variety of models that are available these days, whether you are considering simple, robust models for use on a wargames table; a super-detailed model including interior details in a larger scale; or just a wide collection of different types. Another advantage of armoured car kits in general is that while they may not have some of the attraction/fame of MBTs, they are smaller, less complex and less expensive – so, for the majority of modellers, a more affordable option.

The Airfix Magazine Guide, *a book that prompted my own interest in modelling armoured cars. There is so much more available on the market now than there was then.*

One of my earliest larger-scale models was an armoured car, an Sdkfz 222, and one which actually has a wind-up clockwork motor. It was not brilliantly done but is a model I do still have. I can't actually remember the manufacturer (I think it may have been Nichimo), other than knowing it was an early Japanese kit; plenty more armoured car models under my belt since then, but it still has a place in my collection.

There are models in plastic, white metal or resin, or you can scratch-build your own from a set of scale drawings or, most recently, use a computer to turn those drawings into a 3D model that can then be printed on a 3D printer. As for painting and finishing, I don't claim to give you the most artistic finishes for painting and weathering, but leave that to you to develop as you wish. There are plenty of styles and techniques presented in most commercial modelling magazines, some of which look considerably more 'real' than others. What style to go for is obviously up to each individual modeller. There is also plenty of guidance to be found from manufacturers, such as Ammo by Mig Jimenez and others.

Magazines and websites tend to concentrate on individual subjects, whereas my intention is to provide a much wider perspective on a particular topic, leaving individual modellers to expand their interests and extend their skills in the way they enjoy most. Personally, I build models for my own pleasure, not to win prizes. In the same way I tend not to build dioramas as I just don't have the space for them, so keep just a few bases that I can place models on simply for photographic purposes.

Over many years of modelling, and indeed writing about the hobby, I have so often seen or heard comments from people saying things like, 'I didn't know you could get a model of such and such.' Well, having seen a lot of models over the years, I hope to share with you just how much variety is available within the topic of World War II armoured cars, along with some basic notes on the real things to help with understanding what the models represent, as this might help you choose which ones to try out.

One of my earliest 1/35 models, a clockwork Sdkfz 222, built in the early 1970s.

A selection of armoured car models, all different and in various scales, all of which are covered in this book.

These are all examples of the Sdkfz 263 – in 15mm (1/100), 20mm (1/72), 1/48 and 1/35 scales.

Chapter One

Basic Modelling Equipment

As the aim of this book is to encourage beginners and youngsters to take up the hobby, I will start looking at this aspect of modelling with just the basics, and demonstrate how you can keep costs down and just get on using basic tools. Then I'll move on to a few 'extras', which, while you may not use them every time, are very handy when you do need them. The longer you go on making models, the more tools you are bound to acquire.

BASIC TOOLS

Let's start with what I consider the basic tools needed for building models. These include such things as knives and suchlike, along with materials such as glues.

Modelling/Craft Knives

There is a good mix of different styles of modelling knife on the market. The important thing is to find the style/size of knife handle that is most comfortable to use. I will happily say which ones I have used over the years, but each of us will have our own personal preference. They are not expensive, so you might want to try a few different ones and see which work best for you.

Before I tackle these any further, I must give a safety warning. The blades used with these knives are very sharp indeed. Always be careful how you cut with them: cut away from you, and preferably use with a cutting mat well away from your fingers. Having said that, I still do a lot of clean-up of parts once they are removed from the sprue and that is done in hand. Just be very careful. I have cut myself quite regularly over the fifty-plus years I have been modelling, but never seriously. Even when not serious, however, it is usually painful.

Another safety reminder – especially if you have a young family in the house – is to make sure you don't leave a sharp-bladed craft knife out where it could be picked up by any young children. If you want to encourage any of your children to take up the hobby, train them in the safe use of knives from the very start.

Over the years I have used two particular knives. The older one is the simple Swann-Morton plastic-handled knife, which I find a comfortable fit in the hand; it has several different-style blades (both straight and curved) that are designed to fit it. My preferred blade for years has been their curved No. 2 craft tool blade.

In recent years I have changed to a much smaller, cylindrical metal blade handle, which fits the small Swann-Morton SM065, a straight blade that I find very good for fine work.

Other handle styles include the basic surgical scalpel. This has quite a flat handle and I don't find it comfortable, though the Swann-Morton blades are very sharp indeed. Quite different is

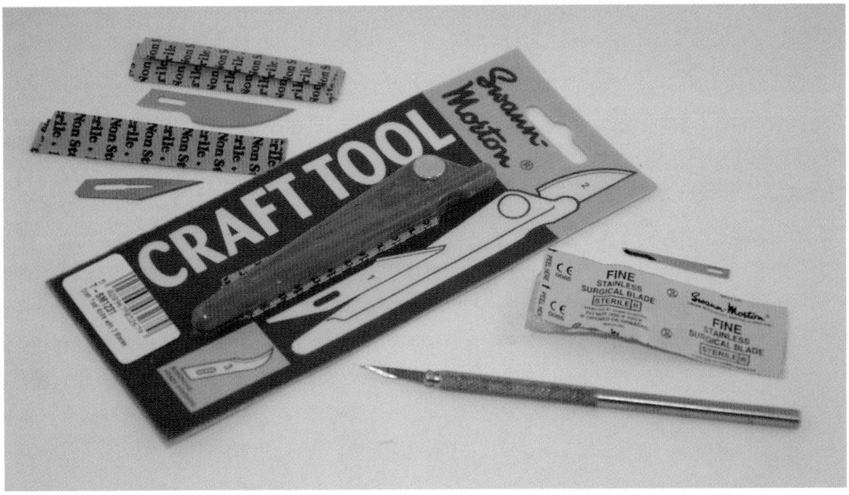

The key tool for modellers, a craft knife. These are my two favourites, but try different ones and choose the type you find most comfortable to use.

the larger-style handle, such as those found on X-Acto tools. Again, I tried these many years ago but found I didn't get on with the larger handle while doing fine work. Try them out and choose your own favourite.

Sprue/Side Cutters

This vital little tool is a 'must have'. You could get by with a pair of scissors but side cutters will make your life much easier. There are various options on the market, but my favourites are in the Xuron range. There have both straight side cutters and the 'shear' type, where the blades overlap very slightly. I use either type when building plastic kits, and they can be useful with resin models as well.

These are more expensive, so if you are on a budget you may find small pairs on sale at market tool stalls for as little as £1; they work well enough, especially given the low price. Equally, I have seen some brands at a considerably higher price point. They may be good but, to my mind at least, not worth the extra cost for what you want them for.

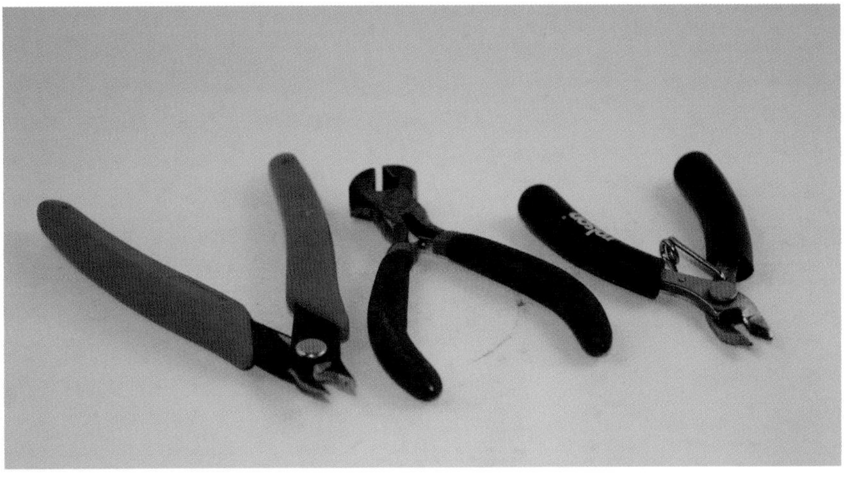

Three different side cutters, another basic tool.

Hand Drill

A pin vice, or hand drill, is a tool I would also put on my 'essential' list. I keep one handy all the time, as they are useful for plastic, resin and metal models. You can buy a great selection of drill-bit sizes, such as in sets as illustrated here. They are not expensive but will last you a long time. The most commonly used drill size is 1mm.

You can buy drills from modelling tool makers such as Revell or Master Tools (a Trumpeter brand), but you can also get them in your local hardware store, and these are usually cheaper. Again, I have found perfectly good drills on sale at market stalls for as little as £1, and at that price it isn't much of a strain to buy two or three if you are concerned they may not last. That said, I have a couple that I have been using for well over thirty years or so.

Files

So-called needle files are handy to have, and generally not expensive. You can also get even smaller ones, referred to as 'rat tail' files, which are handy for sorting out location holes that you may need to drill out to help get a better fit of parts.

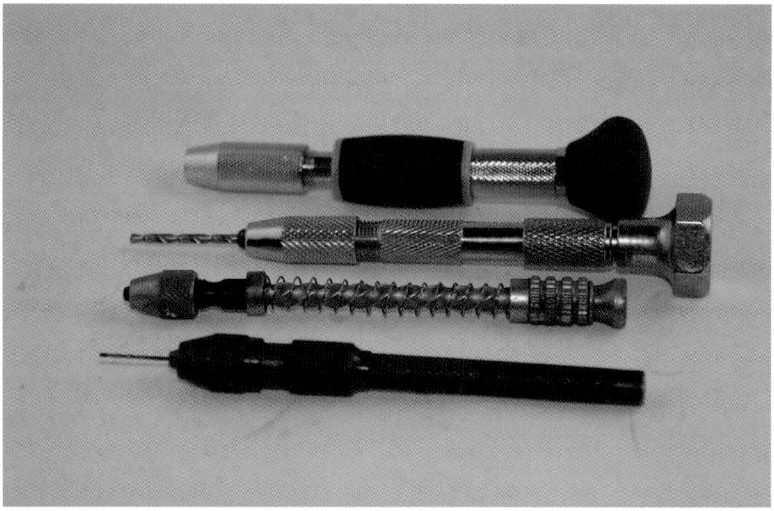

A pin vice is another vital tool for the AFV modeller. They are not expensive and I find I use them on a very regular basis.

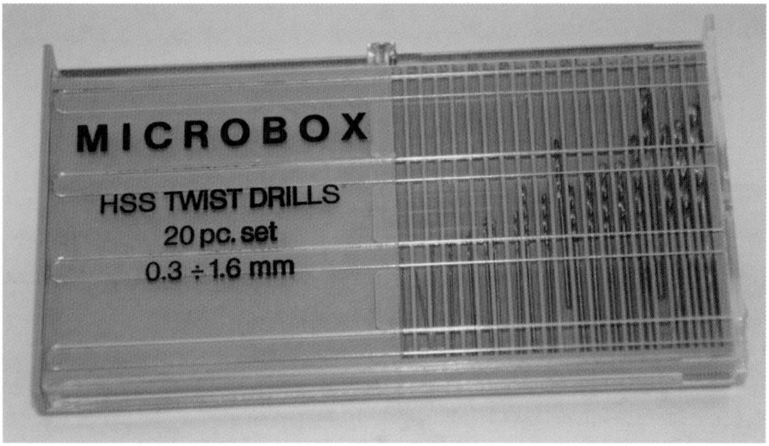

Sets of small-diameter drill bits are readily available and not expensive; the 1mm bit is the one I use most often.

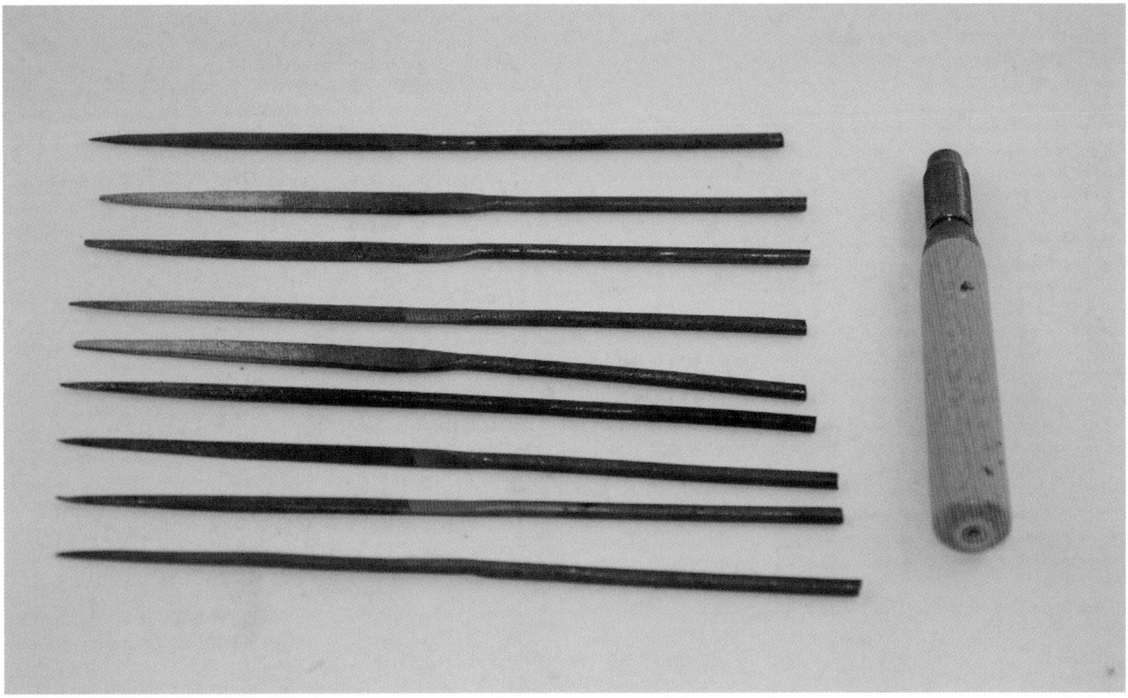

Needle files are very useful to have when the fit of parts need just a little tweaking.

Sanding Sticks

One of the most common issues you will come across in building plastic models is joint or moulding seams. These need to be removed. One way is by careful scraping with a craft knife, but the alternative is to sand them down using a sanding stick. I use both techniques, sometimes in combination. As ever, there is a great variety of types on the market.

They also have different grades of grit. A coarser grit is used for removing a good amount of material, but has the disadvantage that it can leave marks on the plastic bodywork that really you want to leave alone. So, use a finer grit to do the finer work and an almost smooth one for finishing and leaving a smooth surface. A number of companies produce them in the different grades and some also have single sticks with multiple surfaces of different grades all on the one tool. If you look in local chemists', you will find very similar boards (emery boards), sold in the nail care aisles, which can be a handy alternative.

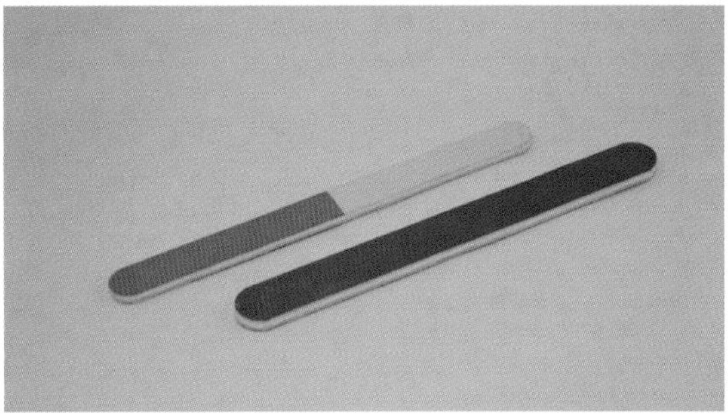

Sanding sticks come in variable grades, from coarse (to remove excess material) to fine (for final finishing/ smoothing).

Razor Saw

A razor saw is a tool I only use occasionally, but when needed, it is the ideal thing. Rather like the basic craft knife, there are various types on the market, with different-size handles and able to hold different grades of blade; which one you go for will come down to personal preference. Yes, price can come into it, but comfort will likely be the deciding factor for any long-term use.

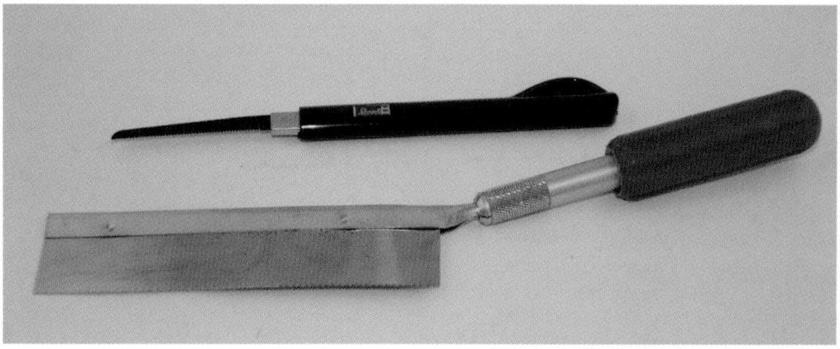

Two different styles of razor saw. Again, try a couple to decide which you prefer.

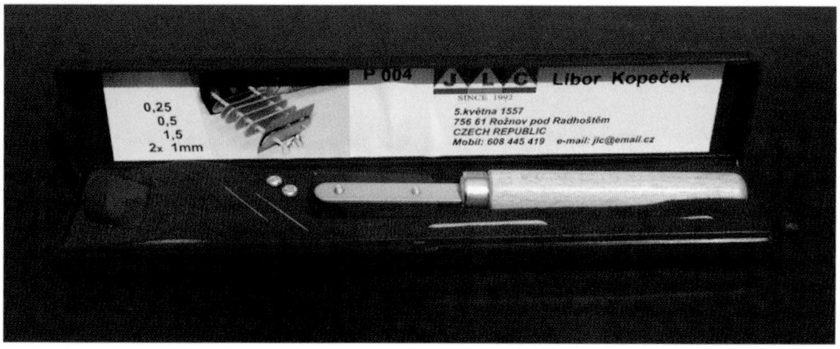

A very fine razor saw from JLC, which makes a finer cut and removes less material, which might affect any new joins.

Tweezers

Another key tool in any modeller's toolbox is tweezers, ideally at least two or three different types. There is a variety on the market, and some come in sets of different styles, for example a straight pair and an angled pair, both with sharply pointed tips. One word of warning with both these is to try not to accidently stab yourself with them, as it hurts (says the voice of experience). These are useful not only when building models but especially for positioning transfers/decals on your completed model.

The slightly larger type of tweezer, with rounder, blunt tips and usually a serrated 'grip' surface, are good for holding model parts, so they don't ping off onto the carpet, never to be seen again.

There is one other style, which uses a crossed structure; with these, a spring design makes them grip for you, rather than your own finger pressure.

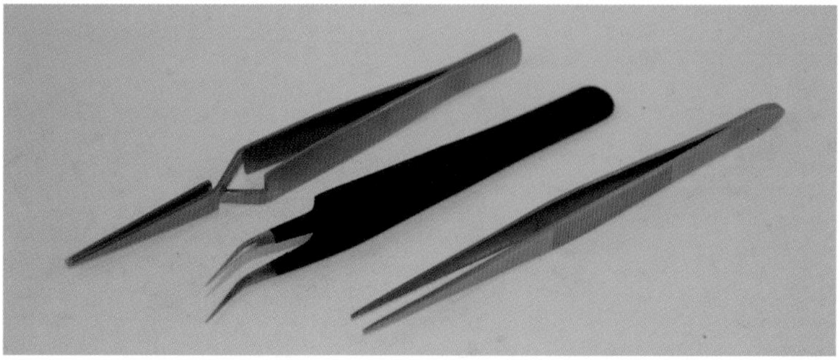

Just three of the many varieties of tweezers, another tool I would not be without.

OTHER MODELLING TOOLS

Metal Ruler

A ruler comes in handy, either 15cm or 30cm, depending on the size of models you like to build. The most important thing to say is to get metal rulers, not cheaper plastic ones. If you are lucky, you can find 'scaled' rulers for 1/76, 1/72, 1/48, 1/35 and so on.

Elastic Bands

Sometimes you will want something to hold larger parts together while the glue dries, for example when building a hull. You can hold parts together in your hands until things 'grip', but sometimes you will get parts that want to spring apart the moment you let go. The simple elastic band can be just the job. You won't need them all that often in my experience, but sometimes plastic parts can become warped for one reason or another, and then they won't fit nice and squarely.

Power Tools

Obviously there are a great many power tools out there with a host of applications. The one I use most is a power drill, in my case a cordless Dremel (I have an older corded one as well, which I keep as a back-up). This is often useful. They also have a wide range of available accessories.

Some power tools come in a small format for modellers, but I have managed to do without these for many years. They include items like a small lathe, sanders and saw tables, which are all available from various manufacturers.

Metal rulers, both 15cm and 30cm, are much better than plastic ones when using a sharp craft knife.

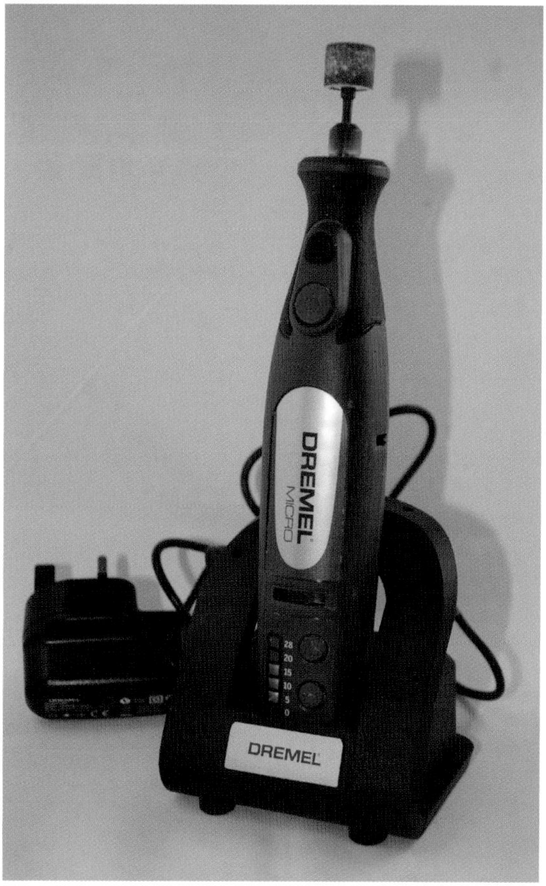

One of the more expensive – but important – tools you might acquire is a cordless power drill, in this case a Dremel.

GLUES AND JOINING MATERIALS

Plastic Cement

We have come a long way from the old tubes that were pretty much the only option when I was young and started modelling, and now there are a number of different makes of plastic cement on the market. They all work essentially the same way, however, melting the surface of the plastic and effectively 'welding' the parts together. It is worth remembering that, and not applying too much in one place, as it can melt/distort the part(s), damaging the surface.

Most of the time these days I use Revell Contacta Professional, which has a long, thin metal applicator tube that helps you apply finely measured amounts of glue to the mating surface of the kit parts. Other brands include the ever-popular Tamiya Extra Thin Cement, which comes in a squat, square bottle, and a brush fixed inside the cap. There is a similar arrangement in Plastic Magic from Deluxe Materials, which I also find very good. Other options are made by the likes of Ammo by Mig Jimenez and Humbrol, to name a couple. I suggest simply trying one or two and deciding which one you like using best.

The one exception is for clear plastic parts – window glazing and periscopes, for example – for which I like the white glues that are usually sold for fixing transparent parts, as these dry clear. The one I use is Glue'n'Glaze from Deluxe Materials. You can use superglue, but be aware this often causes the inside surface to 'fog' and, once fixed inside, you can do little if anything to rectify the problem.

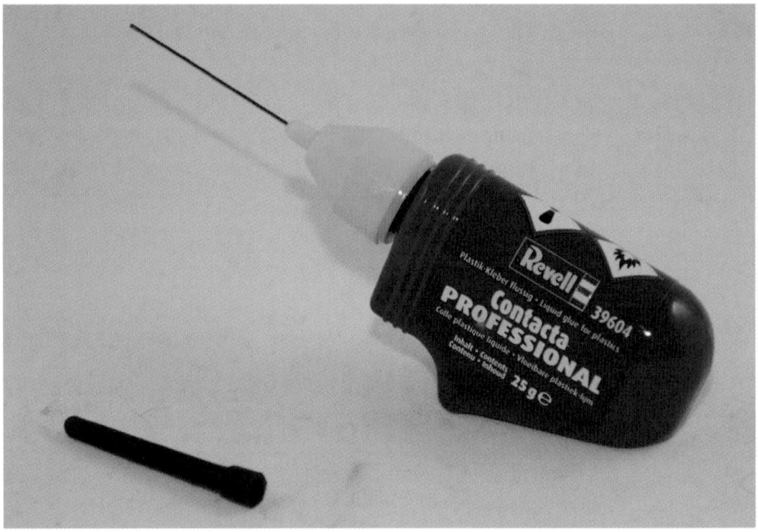

My favourite plastic cement, Revell Contacta Professional, which has a fine metal applicator tube for precise application.

Glue alternatives: the popular Tamiya Extra Thin and Deluxe Materials Plastic Magic.

Superglue

Superglue, or to give it its proper name, cyanoacrylate, is a clear adhesive and a very useful tool for modellers, particularly for assembling both resin and metal models. For a long time I thought that cyanoacrylate glue had been developed as part of the space race, but in reading more about it, I discovered it was actually first developed during World War II in research to make clear plastic gunsights, though it wasn't actually used in the end. After the war, it was not until the 1950s that it was commercially sold as an adhesive, one which quickly gained popularity. It doesn't present a toxic risk, and in fact it is sometimes used in medicine to close a wound as it is quicker than conventional stitches. Fans of crime dramas such as *CSI* will be familiar with seeing it heated inside an enclosed Perspex container to produce fumes, which then stick to the residue of fingerprints, rendering them visible. All in all, it's amazing stuff.

There are a couple of things to note about superglue. It does stick skin very quickly and easily, so do take care when you are using it. Fortunately there are debonding agents available, which I think are very useful to keep handy, just in case. It also has a relatively short shelf-life, about a year from manufacture. I am sure I am not the only one to have gone for a bottle I've kept on one side only to find it set solid. Once it is opened and air gets in, the shelf-life is reduced further, though if you use it regularly then that shouldn't be a problem. Still, this is one reason it tends to be sold in quite small tubes/bottles.

I use superglue for assembling resin models/parts in particular, and also for metal models as an alternative to solder. You can get both thick and thin variations of superglue, each having their particular uses, and most recently, Ammo by Mig Jimenez have introduced one with a black pigment; I must say I have come to like this, simply for being more visible on the parts you have applied it to while you are building your model.

A recent addition to the options for cyanoacrylate is a black version, along with an activator (hardener) from Ammo by Mig Jimenez.

Generally superglue sets very quickly. Bear in mind that a thin layer is generally better than a thick one and sets faster. Sometimes you can find the drying time is a bit slow, and holding parts together accurately while a thicker application sets can be awkward. To help with this, there are hardeners available, which, when applied to the glue, will make it set instantly, providing a good, solid joint. An advantage of this is that you can progress with building the model very quickly, rather than perhaps waiting overnight for a join to dry.

White Glue

White glue, PVA or wood glue is a popular craft product for youngsters and general crafting work. For the modeller it also has some very handy uses. First, and though this is really beyond the scope of this book, I use it for assembling laser-cut MDF-board buildings, which are now widely available from numerous makers, mainly intended for the many structures used on wargames tables, in most popular scales. For the vehicle modeller, it has a couple of particular uses and benefits.

The first of these is to fix transparent parts (window glazing, lights and so on) in place, and the huge benefit of it in this case is that although white glue is a very white colour when wet (so easy to see you have applied it in the right places), it dries clear, so ideal for our purposes. The second use is for etched metal parts, such as engine deck grilles, again because you can easily see where you have applied it and it dries clear. It doesn't dry quite so fast as superglue, so you have that extra bit of time to adjust the positioning of the part(s) before it dries.

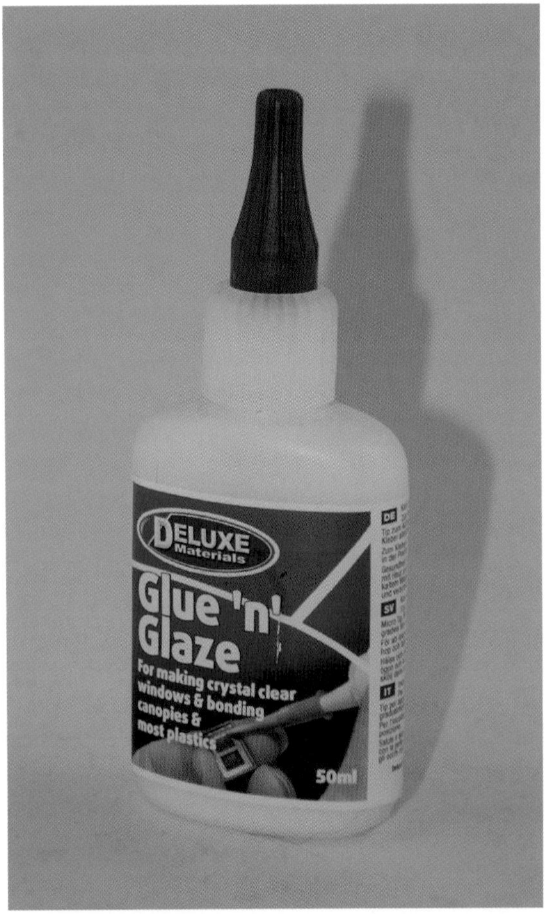

For fixing clear parts, I use Deluxe Materials' Glue'n'Glaze, a white glue that dries clear.

Epoxy Glue

This is commonly used in DIY. It's a two-part material, comprising an adhesive and a hardener in twin packs; the two must be mixed together, usually in a 50/50 ratio, and then applied. It could be used on resin or metal models. Epoxy has the benefit of a good, strong join but has the disadvantages of not only having to get the mix ratio right but also being slow drying. This means that you have time to adjust the positioning of the parts you are joining together, but they then often need to be held/secured in place while it dries. It also tends to create a thicker join, which is not ideal. With the widespread availability of superglues these days, epoxy is now not used so much.

Solder

I think it's fair to say that soldering is not a widely used option for assembling small-scale metal models these days, except maybe by a few for PEB (photo-etch brass). Superglue is a more common choice. I used solder for assembling metal models for some years, but hardly ever now. A soldering iron is not expensive to buy and the more expensive ones come with variable heat settings. You need to use a relatively low-temperature iron along with a flux to help it flow and 'grip' the surface of the metal you are joining. The advantage is a strong join, and in some cases, such as wheels/axles, it can act as a strengthener/reinforcement to the join.

However, the disadvantage is having to work with very hot iron, with its inherent risk of burns; and, unless you are very careful, it is way too easy to apply too much heat to the soft metal parts so that they melt completely, and that really can ruin your modelling day. After a few 'issues' I did get quite well practised at it, but the potential danger of the hot iron with young children in the house, plus fumes from the hot flux and metal when using it, finally led me to stop working with it. Superglue has been my choice for a while now. If you want to find out more about soldering, check the internet for guidance and advice.

Modelling Putty/Filler

Filler is always a handy tool, and something I'd suggest should be a standard part of any modeller's toolbox. There is a variety on the market, including two-part putty (a putty and a hardening compound), such as Miliput or Green Stuff Modelling Compound, and also single-tube materials. My own choices have changed over the years. I used Miliput for many years and it does still have uses, such as moulding sandbags and other stowage items. Once set it can be carved. As a filler, I used a tube of Green Stuff, which works well but you need to be careful not to use too much, and it tends to suffer a bit of shrinkage when it dries. There is even a finer version of the putty, known as 'White Stuff'.

In recent years, I have changed to using Perfect Plastic Putty by Deluxe Materials. It's easy to apply, doesn't shrink and can be sanded once dry without any problems. As always, try some different makes and decide which one you get on with best.

A one-part filler that doesn't shrink, this is Perfect Plastic Putty, also from Deluxe Materials.

STORAGE

Spares Box

One of the things I read about so frequently when I was young was how a modeller used such and such a part from their 'spares box'. Now, in those days I really didn't understand what they meant. Some fifty years or so later I completely appreciate how spare parts build up over the years. So many kits provide optional parts – and this is true of kits in all scales – that if you don't use in a particular build, you can simply save for use another day in another project. How you store yours is up to you; the key thing is, don't throw anything away.

I use the small drawer units that are readily available, and over the years I have got to the point where I have lots of them, filled with all sorts of spare parts and figures.

This is just one of the drawer sets that make up my spares box, an accumulation of bits and pieces from over fifty years of modelling.

A good solution for parts storage, recycled food containers from takeaway restaurants are easily obtainable and free.

Storage Boxes

There is one other cheap and very useful storage resource for modellers, if you are lucky enough to have access to them. Next time you have a takeaway, thoroughly wash out the empty plastic boxes and you effectively have a free storage box complete with lid.

There are all sorts of uses for these. I store partly completed models and parts yet to be fitted in them, keeping everything together, and different sets of wargame figures while they are waiting to be painted. This handy resource is effectively free, as it recycles the plastic rather than simply binning it: a win-win situation, leaving more cash to spend on the hobby itself.

COLOURS AND MARKINGS

Primer

As far as paint for models is concerned, one of the most basic requirements is primer. This is invaluable and, in my opinion, a requirement for resin or metal models and where you have used etched brass. As for a standard plastic kit, you can do without a coat of primer, though my preference these days is still to use it.

When models are cast, they use a mould release agent, such as talcum powder on short-run resin or metal mouldings. The residue from these agents can interfere with the paint finish. One way to get rid of any residue is to wash all the parts in warm, soapy water before you start the build, and then to apply a coat of primer to the built model. You just need to leave clear parts off and fit them after the primer is on, or to mask them before priming.

Once again, there are plenty of different makes of primer on the market in a variety of colours. The main colour I use is grey, but, depending on what colour the final paint scheme will be, sometimes I use white, and you can also use black. I use an acrylic spray can from Halfords, made really for use on cars. These are good value, easy to find in local shopping centres and work really well, providing a smooth, matt surface for your main colours, free from imperfections from any release agent residue.

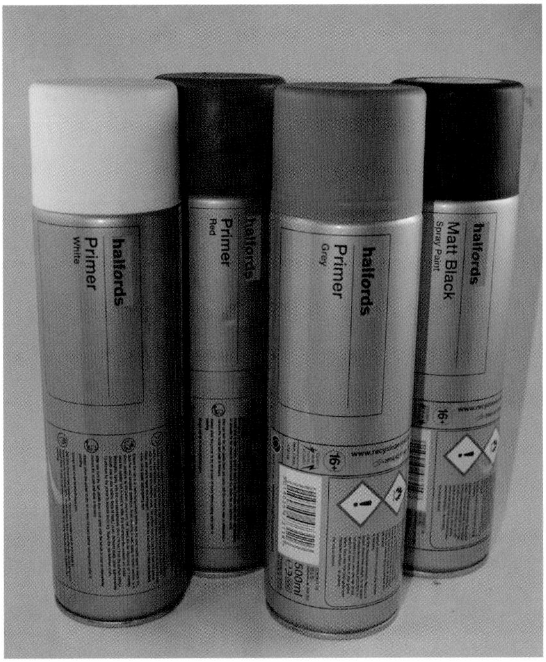

A primer is essential and I use these acrylic sprays from Halfords. They are made primarily for use on cars but are perfect for our hobby too.

Paints and Painting Tools

Most modellers have their own favourite brand of paint so my first suggestion is to try out some different makes and decide for yourself which one(s) you like best. I myself use a variety of different ones, depending on the particular colours I am after. The one big change over my modelling lifetime has been to go from using Humbrol enamels for many years to modern water-based acrylics now. When I started, back in the 1960s, Humbrol enamels were pretty much the only game in town. There were alternatives by Airfix and Revell with their own brands (also enamels) back in the day, but Humbrol really established itself then. In the early 1970s, they upped their game by introducing their 'Authentic Colours' ranges, for aircraft, military vehicles and more. The whole concept of using the right colour matches started to take off in a big way.

Humbrol tinlets alongside their new acrylic pots.

While enamels do dry to a good, tough finish, the smell and need to use a turpentine or white spirit for thinning and cleaning brushes encouraged me to turn to acrylics as they became more readily available, as these have the advantage of using water for thinning and cleaning brushes. I have found brushes last a lot longer too.

One of my favourite acrylics, especially for brush painting, is the range from Italian manufacturer Lifecolor, imported to the UK by The Airbrush Company. Their assorted sets of colours are excellent and I find I get on very well with them. In particular, they do colour sets that include German, Italian and Allied armoured vehicles and I use these a lot. Others that I use regularly are Ammo by Mig Jimenez, AK Interactive and Vallejo. For some particular colours, such as gloss red and orange (for light clusters), I still like to use the modern Humbrol acrylic, while for metallics, the colours from Dark Star are particularly good.

No matter what make of paints you use, the most important lesson I learned over the years is to ensure the pot is thoroughly mixed. Paint left standing in the pot tends to separate, with the pigment settling to the bottom of the pot/jar and the carrier liquid sitting on top. So, before starting, mix the paint by shaking the pot well. Some brands include a ball bearing within the pot to act as an 'agitator', which is a great help. If necessary, be prepared to remove the top of the pot and physically stir the paint, a job I usually do with the handle of an old paint brush.

Oil paints for weathering. These ones are from Abteilung 502.

There is also a place for oil paints, especially for various weathering techniques. I'm not going to explain them here as you can find some perfectly clear guides from manufacturers like AK Interactive, Ammo by Mig Jimenez and others. The excellent Abteilung 502 range and the Oil Brushers from Ammo are just two good brands to look out for.

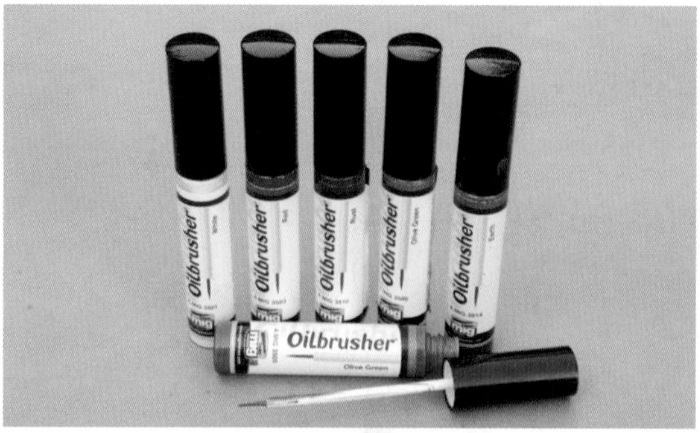

Really easy to use, the Oil Brushers range from Ammo by Mig Jimenez comes in a variety of colours.

Airbrushes

These are great tools, but they can be expensive and they do need to be looked after and cleaned regularly. Airbrushes are available from a number of manufacturers so there are plenty of options, though personally I use Iwata, which has a handy numbering system to classify the different models in their range, and sizes that can cover broader areas or do some very fine linework indeed (although these are more expensive).

You can use canned propellant with your airbrush, but this is an expensive way of doing it if you do a lot of work, so really you want to get a compressor. Again, there is a range of options but price may be a barrier for some. When using an airbrush, you really need a spray booth as well, and to wear a protective face mask/filter.

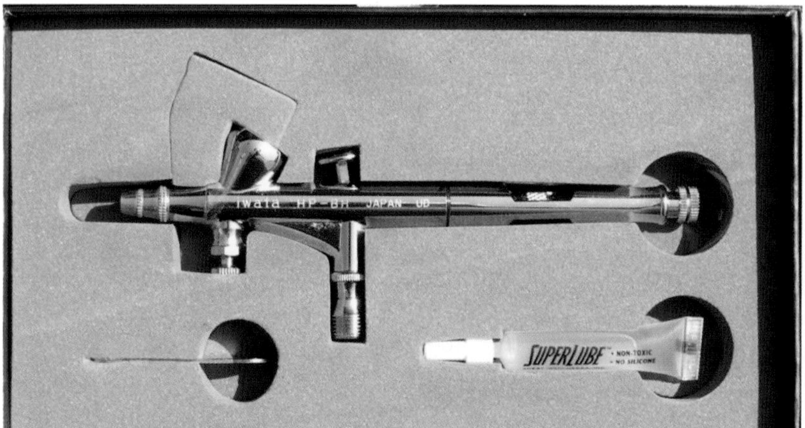

This Iwata Hi-Line airbrush is the one I use for finer lines/camouflage.

If you use an airbrush then you need a compressor. I use this one, a SmartJet Pro from Iwata, available via The Airbrush Company.

Expense, and sometimes personal health issues, mean that airbrush use is not an option for everybody. I often read articles where a modeller talks about using an airbrush as if everyone has one, but while many do, there are plenty who still need to stick with simple brush painting. An airbrush is a 'nice to have' but really not a necessity. I do use one, but that has really only been the case for the last few years, a small part of my modelling lifetime.

Paintbrushes

The humble paintbrush has been my basic paint tool for nearly sixty years, and choosing the right one is important. I know this sounds odd in this day and age, but I never buy paintbrushes over the internet, as I always like to see the individual brush tips that I am buying to ensure they are just right for what I want. Model shows or artist hobby supply stores are my preferred choices, especially for fine-pointed brushes that I use for detail work. You don't want a poorly formed brush, or one where stray hairs are sticking out. Most good makes have a clear plastic protective sheath to protect the head of the brush and I always keep these to protect them when not in use.

The best brushes are made from sable, which is an animal hair, but there are also man-made alternatives, often nylon. The better sable brushes are more expensive but they do get a better finish and give a nice, smooth coat of paint. I especially prefer them for fine, detail painting. The cheaper, synthetic brushes I use more for broader coverage, such as an overall vehicle hull.

As ever, practice will improve your brush skills over time and you will learn your own preferences. I have been modelling for a long time, and, while not the most skilled artist, I have been privileged to have had plenty of comments over the years that models I have brush painted have looked to some as though they had been airbrushed. The right choice of paints and brushes, coupled with plenty of practice, can mean brush painting will give you results just as good as using an airbrush.

A vital tool, the simple paintbrush. This selection shows the variety of size and type of heads you can find.

Palettes

One thing I learned early on in my modelling hobby (back in the days when enamels were really the only game in town), was not to use paint straight from the pot. Always mix it well, either by stirring it, or – with so many modern acrylic paints having a 'dropper'-style cap – by shaking it very well. Then transfer some of the well-mixed paint onto a palette, where it can be used directly or mixed with other colours.

So, what do we use for a palette? You can of course buy paint pallets from many of the major suppliers, such as Humbrol, AK Interactive or Ammo by Mig Jimenez. They are not usually expensive but I have long used a 'free' option, another tiny piece of plastic recycling: I use the old top from the plastic milk containers we buy from the supermarket.

Only dispense enough paint onto the pallet for what you want to do at the time, and just add more if necessary, rather than use too much and end up simply wasting paint.

You can save money and recycle your milk bottle caps as paint pallets.

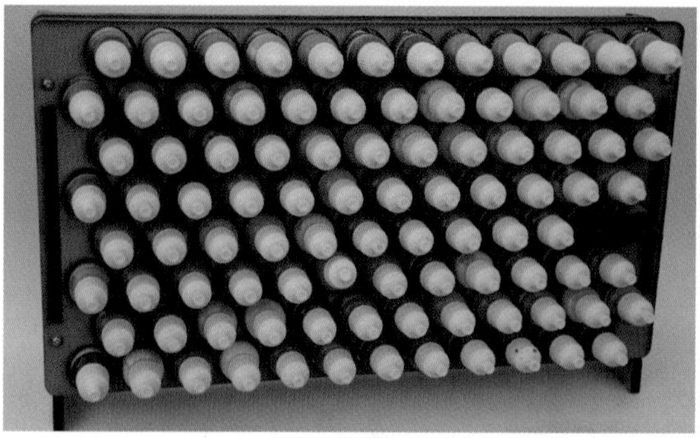

Just one style of MDF paint rack, from Sphere Products.

Paint Racks

It is very easy to build up a large collection of paints as you pursue your hobby, hence it is handy to have some racks to keep them in. For many years I did without, but in recent times there has been a great increase in laser-cut MDF board products, in particular. These are not the only ones, but they have a strength I like. A number of manufacturers produce them these days, but mine are from Sphere Productions, who make specific racks for different-size paint pots, such as Vallejo or Tamiya.

Crocodile Clips

A very handy tool is one that consists of a number of wire supports with crocodile clips to hold parts for you while you paint them, either with a brush or airbrush. You can buy one, but you can also make your own, for not a lot of money. First of all you will need some small crocodile clips. These are inexpensive and can be bought online or in your local hardware/electrical store. Then you need some stout wire. I went for some thick flower-arranging wire. An advantage of this is that the wire is designed to be bent and stay in shape; again, it is not expensive and usually available in a local florist. Staying at the florist, get a block of 'Oasis', a green foam block used in flower arranging. There are two types, and you need the 'dry' rather than 'wet'.

Simply fix a crocodile clip to one end of a piece of wire and use pliers to get them gripped in place. You could reinforce it with superglue if you want

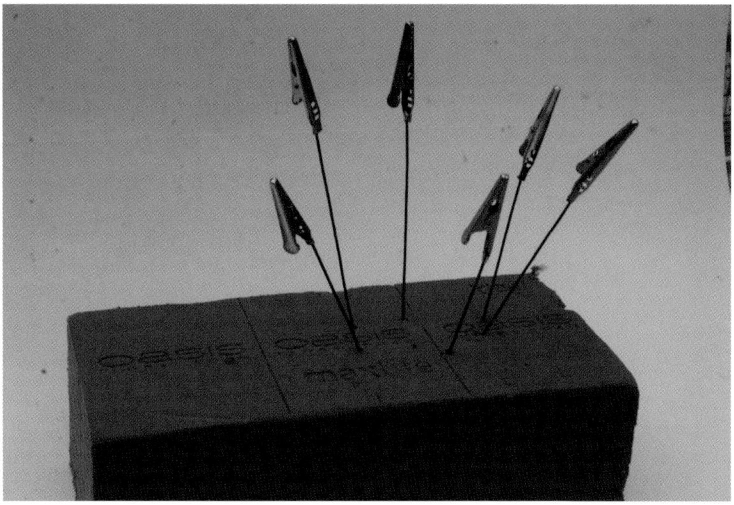

A home-made painting stand, using crocodile clips, some florist's wire and a piece of Oasis, a soft material used in flower arranging.

to, but I didn't bother. Then just stand the wire in the Oasis block. If it becomes loose, simply push the wire into another part of the block. As it gets used, turn the block over and use another of the four large surfaces – it should last quite a while.

Pencil

It may seem odd that I'd mention something as simple as a pencil, but in this case it is not for making notes or drawing plans, but for use on models where you have solid moulded windows. Rather than try to paint glazed windows/vision blocks, I use a tip I picked up many years ago and simply use a soft pencil. This gives not just a grey colour but it also has a shine to it that works well to create the subtle glint of a window and a dark interior without the fuss of painting or using a glossy varnish – not only a good effect, but so easy. The only thing to remember is to keep the pencil sharpened so it can get right into the corners and up to the edges of the frames. I used this on the windows of a small, solid resin model of an armoured Kubelwagen that you will see in Chapter 3.

Correct Colours

The debate about the 'right' shade of colour for this or that has been batted around among modellers for many years. I don't want to get embroiled in that argument as there are plenty of firmly held views out there. The most common issue concerns the 'right' shade of Olive Drab.

My own view is that there is no right answer. During World War II, there were huge demands for military vehicle production in all countries involved in the war, and therefore a need to paint them. So multiple manufacturers, even if working to the same basic specifications, had to get their own raw material supplies and mixes. There were no computer-controlled machines to do it for them, just people who needed to get some paint made and out of the factory door. Once the paint got to the vehicle manufacturing plants it would be applied, perhaps with different primer coats (maybe none, in some Russian factories close to the fighting) and not by people worrying about whether it was the right shade. The result will have been a good deal of variation in colour between vehicles. Even today, if you look at any parking area filled with military vehicles, you will see that use, weather conditions and age of the paint will have changed the colours considerably from one vehicle to another. Furthermore, if vehicles had been into field workshops during their time in service, all sorts of extra variations are likely to have been introduced, thanks to repairs or replacement parts. The technicians will have focused on getting the vehicle back into action rather than matching the paint correctly.

One of the best examples I can think of to illustrate this point is the late-war German camouflage scheme, where the vehicle usually came in a coat of plain dark yellow (Dunkelgelb) and tins of paste with green (Dunkelgrün) and red-brown (Rotbraun) camouflage colours that could be applied by individual units (even individual crews), depending on the conditions they were in at the time. The pastes could be mixed with petrol for a lasting colour, or water if petrol was in short supply, though that could lead to it being washed off in heavy rain. The variations in that local mixing led to light and dark variations of both the greens and red-browns that could be down to individual crews, so I think it is fair to say there is no 'correct' version.

In short, there are plenty of references (*see* below) to guide you to the right colours for particular vehicles at particular times and places during the war, but there's no need to get too hung up over the exact shade of colour. It will be altered by any weathering you apply to it anyway, so decide for yourself what you feel looks right and what you are happy with.

Good references to give you an idea of what the 'right' colours are for German vehicles are the three volumes of *Panzer Colours*, produced by both Squadron-Signal and Arms & Armour press. For British colours, there is no better reference than the series of booklets by Mike Starmer; for the available list of titles and costs, you can email him at mike_starmer@hotmail.com.

Transfers/Decals

When I started modelling in the early 1960s, we referred to these as transfers; only later did the term 'decal' become popular. Technically there may be a difference between the two, but for the modeller they are essentially the same thing and both terms are in common usage.

Over the years there have been two or three different styles but by far the most common are 'waterslide'. The printed designs are on a backing paper, which you soak in lukewarm water to release the individual transfer and then apply

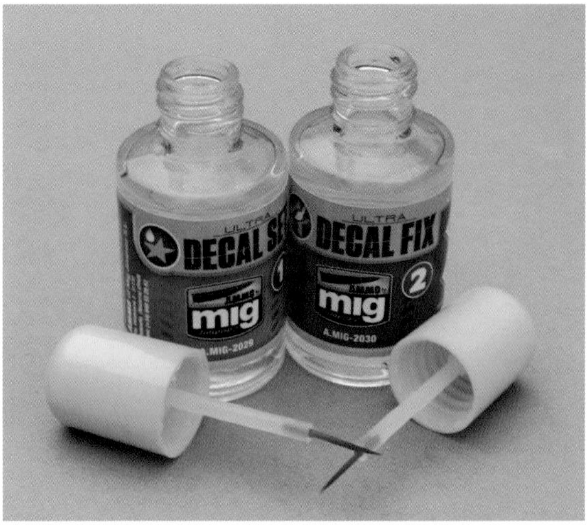

Solutions to help in the application of transfers: a setting and a fixing solution, in this case from Ammo by Mig Jimenez.

it to your model. It can be a simple as that, but sometimes you may experience issues, such as air bubbles trapped under the transfer or the clear edge of it producing a 'shine' that can spoil the finished model.

It is therefore advisable to use setting solutions to help eliminate the potential issues. These are also a great help in getting the designs to sit tightly over raised detail, such as bolt heads. Soak off the individual transfer in water, and separately paint the setting solution onto the model with a brush. Apply the transfer and adjust the position to get it just right, then use a cotton bud or soft cloth to press it down, forcing excess water or air out from beneath it. Then apply the fixing solution and again use a cotton bud or cloth to remove any excess. This may need some practice, as if you use too much of these solutions then the decals become so soft that they wrinkle up too much and are effectively ruined.

Vehicle Markings

The assortment of markings seen on military vehicles in use by the various nations is a subject all by itself, and well beyond the scope of this book, although you will find some useful reference books in the bibliography. I will make a couple of comments, though, relating the topic of markings to the preceding topic of transfers.

The first is that most plastic kits include an appropriate set of markings for individual vehicles and in most cases have spares for other options. Once you have used the right ones for your chosen finish, make sure you keep all the remainder. You will soon build up a good collection of spares, which you can turn to when you decide to build a resin or metal model, many of which do not come with their own transfers. This applies whatever your preferred scale.

The second is to mention the availability of aftermarket sets of transfers/decals. I have never felt that the AFV modeller is as well served in this regard as aircraft modellers, but there are actually a few very useful sources. My earliest memories are the old Almark Transfers of the late 1960s/ early 1970s. These days there is a wide range available in small scales thanks to The Plastic Soldier Company, who make them in both 15mm (1/100) and 20mm (1/72) scales. There are also small-scale sets produced by Skytrex and by Mike Starmer. Star Decals makes a wide assortment of sets in 1/72, 1/48 and 1/35 scales, and more 1/35 sets are available from Echelon and Accurate Armour – and not just for armoured cars. Then, from the USA, in both 1/72 and 1/35 scales, there is a huge range by Archer Fine Transfers. Archer started out making dry-rub transfers but these are now being changed over to conventional waterslide types instead. If you combine your transfer spares box with a selection of aftermarket packs, you should find plenty to keep you busy.

Chapter Two

British and Commonwealth Armoured Cars

BRITISH UNITS

Humber Scout

Let's start with one of my personal favourites. The Humber Scout Car 4×4 was in production from 1942 through to 1945, and over 4,100 were made. It came in Mk I and Mk II iterations, which were essentially similar, but the Mk II is recognizable by having a slight hump added in the armour just in front of the driver's position to allow some more room above the steering wheel. It was a light scout car built by the Rootes Group for the same requirement as the very successful Daimler Dingo, needed because Daimler simply couldn't build enough to meet demand.

Unlike the Dingo, the Humber did have an enclosed crew compartment, with two sliding hatches for the crew in the roof plate. Only lightly armoured, it protected the two-man crew against small arms fire but was only intended for reconnaissance and liaison duties, not as a front-line fighting vehicle. It was lightly armed, with a single, or sometimes a twin, Bren gun mounting on the roof, which could be operated remotely from within the crew compartment without the crew member having to be exposed outside the vehicle. Having said that, they would have had to do so when the magazines on the Bren(s) needed to be replaced. Perhaps the most famous appearance of a Humber is in the film *A Bridge Too Far*, the story of Operation *Market Garden*, when Michael Caine is seen riding in one as Lt Col. J.O.E. Vandeleur, who commanded the 3rd Battalion Irish Guards and who led the advance of 30 Corps towards Arnhem.

The Humbers were used by British armoured units in the Northwest Europe campaign as well as being supplied to Polish and Czech units. After the war they were used by other European countries, such as Belgium. Quite a number of Humbers survive in both museums and private ownership, so they can be seen quite regularly at military vehicle rallies.

For the modeller, there is plenty of choice as the Humber has been quite popular with manufacturers over the years. Accurate Armour first produced a 1/35 resin model, which is very nice though with a solid resin body and does look good. More recently, Bronco Models have produced a plastic kit of the Humber that also includes the internal details of the crew and engine compartments, along with crew figures.

This is a classic example of how for years we largely relied on resin model producers for subjects that frankly we never imagined we might see in plastic. In the last ten years or so that situation has changed, as a number of manufacturers, especially from the Far East, have been producing new models at an amazing rate. New technology for design and production of injection-moulded models has advanced and at the same time has reduced the time and cost of making new production moulds. These days we see new kits released at a rate that I could only have dreamed of when

This is the Accurate Armour 1/35 resin model of the Humber Scout Car.

Box art for the Bronco kit. This kit includes crew figures.

I was younger. That in turn has undoubtedly hit the sales of those resin-model producers who bolstered our hobby over many years.

In the smaller scale of 1/76, I remember that the Humber was one of the first metal models in the MMS range in the 1980s, when Barry Walby created a new metal model from a resin version he had originally made back in the early 1970s. There have also been resin models, including one from Milicast. More recently, we have seen another development that I think of as significant. Cottage industries, where enthusiasts have produced their own range of resin or metal models, are mostly just one-person operations, without the large-scale financial backing of bigger business. For these, it is a significant jump to invest in production of an injection-moulded plastic kit.

One business that has made that leap is Dan Taylor Modelworks, who has invested in the production of a 1/72 injection-moulded kit of the Humber Mk I and Mk II Scout Car. More to the point, the kit is excellent and assembles very well, including internal details for the crew compartment and a choice of markings. I believe we should support the venture by buying the kit as this is the only way we can pay back the risk taken in the original investment and enable new kits later on.

The recent 1/72 kit of the Humber from Dan Taylor Modelworks.

The built but unpainted 1/72 Dan Taylor model.

The completed Dan Taylor model, painted and with markings applied.

Daimler Dingo

The Daimler Dingo was designed in 1938, just before the start of World War II, to meet a requirement for a light liaison/scout armoured car. The winning design came from BSA Cycles, rather than the other two contenders, Alvis and Morris. Oddly, it was the Alvis design they had called the Dingo, while the successful BSA design was known more formally as 'Car, Scout, Mk I'. The actual production of the vehicle was passed to Daimler, another part of the BSA Group, who went on to produce large numbers of what became known as the Dingo, and which turned out to be a very successful design.

A small, compact, four-wheel-drive vehicle with a crew of two, the Dingo had a good turn of speed in either direction, thanks to a clever gearbox design that allowed for five speeds both ways. Early examples even had four-wheel steering, which gave it a good, tight turning circle but proved troublesome for some drivers to manage. The later versions, and the bulk of the 6,626 that were built, reverted to just front-wheel steering.

Another unusual feature was in the seating arrangement. The driver had his seat angled slightly so he could more easily turn his head and see out of a secondary visor in the body armour behind his head if he needed to drive the Dingo backwards, making good use of the speed from those five reverse gears. At the same time, the second crew seat could revolve, allowing the second crewman/commander to operate the Bren gun or Boys anti-tank rifle that could be mounted in front, or turn to use the No. 19 wireless behind him.

The Dingo was open-topped, though it did have a cover. On the early versions this was a sliding one, but it was changed to a folding arrangement for the majority. These later models also had seat pads so a commander/observer could sit that bit higher and get a clearer view while on patrol.

All in all, the Dingo was small, fast, reliable, had good mobility and was fitted with 'run-flat' tyres that were almost solid, so did not need to carry a spare wheel. It proved a reliable and popular vehicle that went on to serve with many nations around the world long after the end of World War II. There were also a couple of copies, one from Canada and the other from Italy, which I'll deal with separately. These days, the Dingo is popular with private owners and is frequently seen at military vehicle shows.

Dingos Today

Seen at the War and Peace show at Beltring, Kent in 2009 and 2013, two different restored Dingos are a good example of how the interior of this open-top car has the same basic colour inside as out. The only other colours are the wood stock of the Bren gun armament, extra magazines, the canvas seats, the radio, tucked away behind the commander's seat and other detail fittings.

Front view of a Daimler Dingo at the War and Peace show in 2013.

Rear view of the Dingo.

Being an open-top vehicle, the interior colour is the same as the exterior. This is the driver's position and the stock of the Bren gun is visible on the left-hand side of the picture.

The second crew position, with stowed gear in set spots as indicated by the stencilling. Notice the spare magazines for the Bren gun on the right and the spare Bren barrel.

The radio fitted behind the passenger seat.

The fuel tank is the largest item behind the driver's seat.

When I started modelling in the 1960s, the idea of scratch-building certain armoured vehicles with multi-faceted armour plates was too daunting. So I was delighted when two early Dingo kits became generally available. One was an early 1/35 kit by Tamiya and the other was the 1/76 model from Matchbox, which came paired with 'Monty's Caravan', a Leyland Retriever truck with a special office body used by Field Marshal Montgomery. This truck was one of three specialist vehicles used by Monty. He kept the originals at his home after the war, saying they were his rather than the army's, though when he passed away they were left to the Imperial War Museum, who have kept them on display first at Lambeth and now at their IWM Duxford site.

Appropriate though it was to have a liaison vehicle coupled with the command caravan, I suspect I am not the only modeller who bought multiples of the kit more for the Dingo than the Leyland Retriever. There are many other body types that can be fitted to that cab and chassis combination, but they lie outside the scope of this book so will have to wait for another time.

The Dingo built very neatly and got the right look to this little armoured car. Sadly, Matchbox went out of business many years ago, but the good news is that their moulds were bought up by Revell, who re-release these kits, including Monty's Caravan and the Dingo, on a fairly regular basis. You should therefore still be able to find these readily available in the shops and at a very reasonable price for what you get. Revell small-scale armour comes in two scales. Their own, often new subjects, are in 1/72, while all the old Matchbox kits are still correctly marked up as 1/76. One other little extra with these old models is that they all include a small diorama base as well.

The Tamiya kit, in 1/35, is an old model now, but still basically right. It has a couple of crew figures with it and is a simple, straightforward kit to build. As with all Tamiya models, the fit of parts is excellent so this will be a quick one to put together.

Tamiya actually have another Dingo kit in their range, this time in 1/48. They originally started a series of 1/48 AFV models many years ago, but they didn't take off and the range wasn't expanded. It is only in more recent years that we have seen that change, and an extensive range of World War II military vehicles has been regularly added to their list of 1/48 models that has proved to be very popular indeed. Perhaps it's no surprise that they have included a Dingo in this new scale as well then. Again, this model has excellent fit of parts and is easy to build, and includes two crew figures.

The completed Tamiya 1/48 Dingo, complete with crew figures.

MiniArt box art for their 1/35 Dingo Mk III with crew.

Used in France in 1940, and in North Africa as well as Italy and Northwest Europe after D-Day, the Dingo came in a good variety of colour schemes, leaving you many options both for disruptive camouflage and single colour schemes. In more recent times, MiniArt, a company based in the Ukraine, have done some variations on their Dingo kit, and these come with excellent detail both inside and out.

Bedford OXA

The Bedford OXA was another emergency design produced in the early stages of World War II, prompted by the defeat of the BEF in France in 1940 and the real threat of a German invasion of the UK. It was based on the 1.5-ton chassis of the Bedford OXD truck, with armour panels to protect the engine and cab, plus a new, simple box body. It was armed with a Boys anti-tank rifle.

A 1/72 resin model of the Bedford OXA, available only to current members of MAFVA.

The OXA was a very basic armoured truck, but it was created when it was badly needed, after so much equipment had been left behind in France when the BEF was forced into the evacuation at Dunkirk. Bedford built 948 of these; they were used by British regular army units and were later transferred to the Home Guard.

The OXA was one of the models scratch-built in the old Airfix book, but as far as models are concerned now, there have been kits in 1/35 from MMK, 15mm wargame scale from Flames of War, and – for Braille scale fans – there is a 1/72 scale resin model available only to members of MAFVA (Miniature Armoured Fighting Vehicles Association). I will take this chance to encourage any military vehicle modeller to join this organization.

Standard Beaverette

The Standard Beaverette Mk I was a rather primitive armoured car. Like the OXA, it was first designed and built in 1940 as a rather desperate measure to help reinforce the UK at a time when there was a real fear of a German invasion, and was issued to the Home Guard, the army and RAF for airfield defence. Using a commercial two-wheel-drive chassis built by the Standard Motor Company, it added a lightly armoured body that was open both on the top and at the rear, with a slit in the front plate for fitting a Bren gun (or potentially a Boys anti-tank rifle). The thin armour was backed on the inside with wooden planks and the front wings were still from the basic civilian car it was based on. Visibility for the driver, through a small slit in the armour, was very restricted, so they often had to rely on guidance from an observer standing in the car. The Mk II was very similar, but did have the armour extended around the back of the body although it still had an open-top roof.

The Beaverette Mk III was a bit different. This had a shortened chassis (3.1m on the Mk III compared to 4.11m on the Mk I) and a completely new, simplified and fully enclosed armoured body along with a small turret for the Bren gun armament on the roof.

A production figure of 2,800 for all marks is given for the Beaverettes, and production ended in 1942. It was used for training and UK defence purposes only.

I remember as a youngster visiting an aunt and uncle in Berkshire. A short walk from their house near Aldermaston were the remains of an old Beaverette Mk III, minus the turret, axle deep in the ground and hidden under trees at the edge of

This real example of the Beaverette Mk III can be seen at the IWM (Imperial War Museum) Duxford, Cambridgeshire.

A one-piece metal 1/76 model of the Beaverette Mk I.

Rear view of the Beaverette Mk I.

The Beaverette Mk III, a 1/76 resin model by Gramodels.

a wood. It's probably long gone, but the Imperial War Museum (IWM) site at Duxford has a beautifully restored example of this little armoured car on display in one of the hangars, amid the aircraft that they were once used to protect.

I have a 1/76 metal model of a Standard Beaverette Mk I that is a simple one-piece casting.

As for the Beaverette Mk III, there is a nice little resin model in the Gramodels range. This is a simple model and easy enough to build. All you need to find is a Bren gun to fit in the turret. For mine, I used a metal-cast one that is available in an accessory pack of British infantry weapons from Sgts Mess, a wargames model manufacturer who also have a very useful range of small-scale metal accessory packs.

Though I haven't seen the kits themselves, there are also 1/35 models of both the Beaverette Mk I and the Mk III listed in the range from IMA (International Models Asia) Co.

Humber LRC (Light Reconnaissance Car)

Another 4x2 armoured car based on a car chassis, this one used the Humber Super Snipe, from part of the Rootes Group. The basic car itself was famously used by Montgomery in the civilian-pattern open-top version, while there were also hard-top saloons and the military unarmoured Humber Heavy Utility. Given a fully armoured body, it became the Humber LRC. Around 3,600 were built between 1940 and 1943. The first few had an open-top hull but that was quickly replaced with the Mk II, which had an armoured roof and a small turret for either a Bren gun or Boys anti-tank rifle. The Mk III looked pretty much the same, but importantly had four-wheel drive; it went into production in 1941. A Mk IIIA was produced from 1943, and this had some additional vision ports.

The Humber was operated by infantry reconnaissance regiments and the RAF, and served in North Africa, Italy and Northwest Europe. Out of interest, there were some special versions made, such as the 'Ironside Special Saloon', with a side door and more comfortable interior seating, which were built for use by the royal family and cabinet ministers, plus some used as senior command vehicles.

A number of the Humber LRCs served on after the war, including in India and the Far East, and some preserved examples can be seen at military vehicle rallies such as the War and Peace show to this day.

There have been a few small-scale models of the Humber over the years, in both metal and resin. The metal model I like was done by MMS Models, a 1/76 range created by my long-time friend Barry Walby. The MMS range is not currently in production, but I know it has been purchased by a new owner who will be getting it back into production, hopefully starting in 2021. In the meantime, look out for any offered on eBay or similar auction sites. Another option is a polyurethane resin model from Milicast, also in 1/76.

I believe there are 1/35 resin models of both the Humber LRC Mk I and the Mk III available from IMA (International Models Asia), and though I haven't seen the kits myself, IMA do have a very good reputation.

A Humber LRC seen at the War and Peace show at Beltring, Kent, in 2007.

Two small-scale Humber LRC models. On the left is a metal kit from MMS, and on the right a resin kit by Milicast.

A completed resin model of the Humber LRC.

Morris LRC

Morris were another British car maker brought in to build a light reconnaissance car, and they made 2,200 of them between 1940 and 1944. Quite a small, compact 4×2 armoured car, the Morris version was unusual for having the three crew sitting side by side – the driver in the centre, with the other two either side serving a Bren gun in the small turret on the driver's right and a Boys anti-tank rifle fitted in the raised hatch cover on the left. Like the Humbers, they served in North Africa, Italy and Northwest Europe. There are surviving examples at both the IWM Duxford in Cambridgeshire, and at the Tank Museum in Bovington, Dorset.

Building a Morris LRC

This is a good opportunity to go through a build, using the Morris LRC by Accurate Armour, a 1/35 kit in polyurethane resin. This is quite simple in terms of the number of parts so is a great choice for a new or inexperienced modeller.

The first step is to open up the box and check all the parts. This is easy enough thanks to a full parts list, which Accurate Armour include as standard in their assembly instruction leaflets. With resin models, it is worth checking all the parts at this stage to make sure everything has been moulded correctly. Though it is much less common these days, resin casting can leave blemishes/holes caused by air bubbles. With Accurate Armour kits this is rarely a problem, as they use a vacuum casting system that eradicates any air bubbles. However, it is a good habit to always check, and if you do find a problem that can't be simply filled, contact the supplier and request a replacement part.

With everything ready to proceed, the next step is to wash all the parts in a mild soapy solution. This ensures that any release agent (used to enable the parts to easily come away from the moulds) left from the casting process is removed, something that can spoil things when you come to paint the model. Leave the parts to dry thoroughly before starting the build. For the assembly I am going to use superglue, or cyanoacrylate.

There are a couple of important safety points to bear in mind. One is that polyurethane resin is thought to be a carcinogen, so care needs to be taken – nothing extreme, just basic precautions. In its moulded state it is completely harmless. What you need to be careful of is any dust particles that could be released while cleaning up the parts ready for assembly. For this reason, the one thing *not* to do with resin is to use a power tool to sand down the excess resin. That would create far too much fine dust that you

Box art for the Accurate Armour Morris LRC.

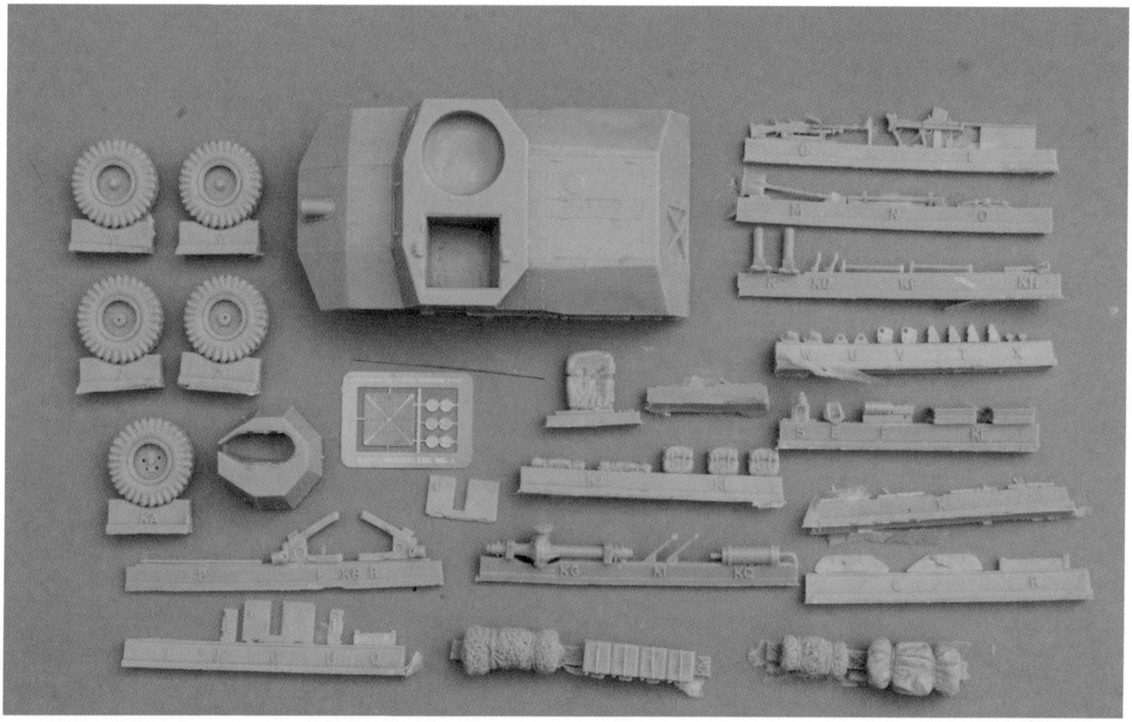

Parts layout for the Accurate Armour kit.

could inhale. If you do want to sand something down, use wet and dry paper and do it in water, or outside and wearing an appropriate protective mask (the sort of thing you might wear for DIY tasks around the house).

Second – and this applies to building a plastic kit as well – it is advisable to wear some protective goggles, as it is all too easy for a small piece of excess resin to fly up into your eye. I know that might sound extreme, but it comes from experience; I have had a couple of narrow escapes over the years from getting complacent.

Major parts, such as the hull in this case, can be checked over for any signs of excess resin on the edges, which can simply be cleaned off with a sharp craft knife. On this kit that was a very minor issue indeed, and quickly and easily done on the looser edges of the bodywork.

All the smaller parts are moulded on a length of 'carrier', from which they need to be carefully removed. Helpfully, the carrier also has individual part identification letters on it that tie in with the parts list, enabling you to check all the parts are there and identify the right ones during the build process.

To free these casting runners/blocks, I use a pair of side cutters to remove the large parts, and then a craft knife to *carefully* cut or scrape down any remaining excess. For smaller parts, such as the lifting eyes and rear lights in this case, use a sharp craft knife to score along the edge, on both front and back; the part will then snap away. If it doesn't go easily, score it again – very carefully, so you don't slip and cut yourself with the sharp blade. Clean up the edges, which will then be glued to the main bodywork.

Now you are ready to get on with building the model. Accurate Armour does supply a good set of illustrated assembly instructions, combining notes and photos of the model parts as you go.

The build starts with the front suspension. The photos show these parts as metal castings, but in the kit they are actually in resin. The main wishbones and spring suspension parts are easy to fit, and there is a locating hole for the spring in the hull casting so they go together easily in the right place. Add the steering rods and tie rods (from wire provided) and then the rear axle and short driveshaft, which again locate very simply. Don't add the wheels yet.

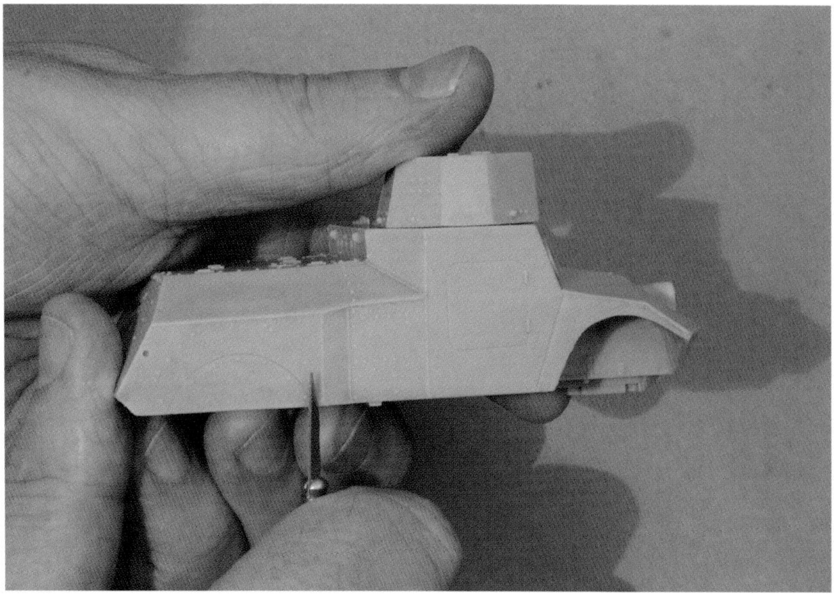

Underside of the Morris kit under construction.

The next step is to start adding the details to the hull itself. These include the lifting eyes at both front and back of the hull, along with the small light fittings, also front and back. You also now get to choose how you want to fit the hatches for the two crew positions, the driver and the gunner/ commander in the small turret. I chose to have these open, even though the hull is moulded solid, so there is no interior to be seen. At some point I will add a couple of crew figures, but there aren't any included in the kit.

There are just a couple of pieces of etch brass in this kit, put to ideal use for the wing mirrors and the mesh screen over the fan on the back plate of the hull. Personally, I choose to add these right near the end, once the hull has been primed and painted, but before adding any markings and weathering. This saves the wing mirrors being knocked off while you are still handling the model in the building process.

The other elements included with this kit are some stowage items. These include fuel cans, boxes, rolled ground sheets and camouflage nets. The instructions show these fitted around the rear engine deck, but you can choose which to use and how to suit your own plan.

The instructions show the rear axle being fitted in the first stages. Very unusually for me, I followed the assembly sequence given in the instructions, but I later wished I had done it slightly differently. Unlike the front wheels, the rear wheels are half covered by the armoured body. With the axles already fixed in place, it is a very tight fit to get the rear wheels in place on the axle stubs. Resin is a little forgiving, so I did get them in successfully, but if I was doing it again I would fit the wheels to the rear axle and then fit that complete assembly onto the underside of the hull.

With the build essentially completed, apart from the wheels, the two weapons and the etch screen, the next thing to do is give it a coat of primer. Again, there's lots of choice here, but my preferred choice is a grey acrylic spray paint from Halfords. I don't do this in the house, but using an old box, spray it outside, as I am lucky enough to have a shed in the garden. Just do it in thin passes, taking care not to apply too much paint all together, and then leave it to dry, which is actually very quick.

Once the primer was dry, I chose to brush paint the Morris and used British Olive Drab SCC15 from the Lifecolor Paints set, British Tanks, Set 2, ref LC-CS44, plus Dirty Black, another Lifecolor Paint from their Shades of Black set, LC-CS27, for the tyres. The Boys and the Bren were done with a Citadel paint colour, Abaddon Black.

The kit built and ready for a coat of primer.

The primed kit. The wheels and guns will be fitted once the wheel wells have been painted.

The Morris kit with primer applied.

Views of the completed Morris LRC model.

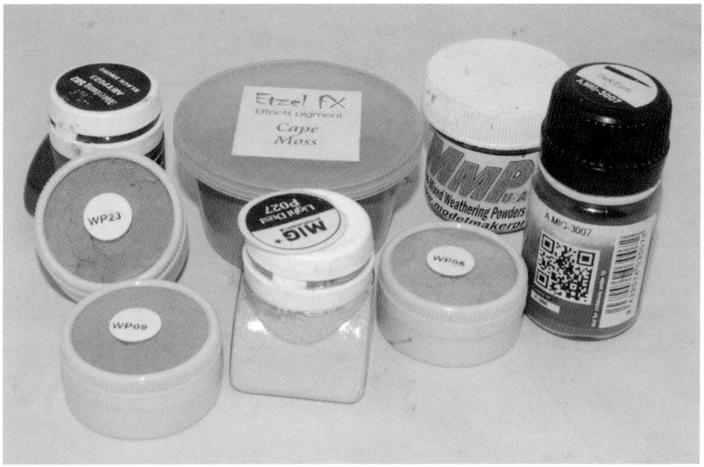

There is a wide variety of makes and colours for weathering pigments.

Views of the completed Morris LRC model.

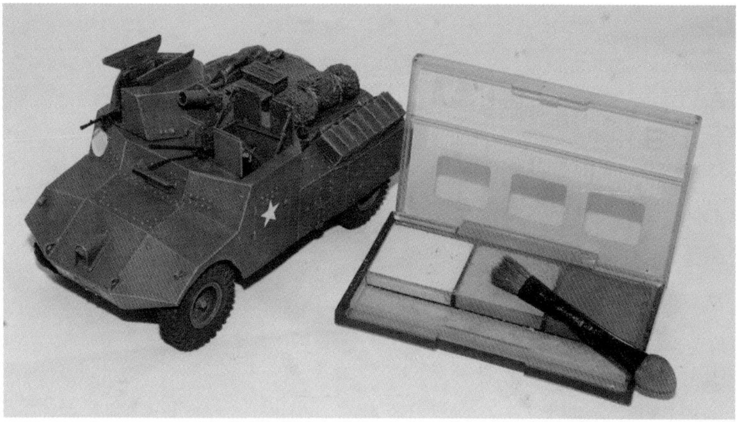

With the Morris painted and transfers applied, the next thing is to highlight the details by brushing the model with a light-green pigment. I used one of the Tamiya sets of Weathering Powders, applied with the brush that comes in the pack.

Highlighting like this was in the past often done by dry brushing, but in recent years I much prefer the more subtle finish you get from pigments.

As a final touch, add some light weathering, effectively a coat of dust. Again, this is done by applying pigment, applied/rubbed in using an old brush.

Morris CS9

Another armoured car from British motor manufacturer Morris, the CS9 was based on the 4×2 chassis of the Morris Commercial C9, a 15cwt truck chassis. It was fitted with a riveted hull and an open-top turret, which carried the armament of a Boys anti-tank rifle and a Bren LMG. Importantly, it also mounted a No. 19 radio set. It carried a crew of four (commander, driver, gunner and radio operator) and weighed in at 4.5 tons.

After the prototype was tested in 1936, an order was placed for another ninety-nine, which were delivered in 1938. The 12th Royal Lancers took thirty-eight of them to France as part of the BEF, but they were all lost in the fighting that led to the Dunkirk evacuation. Thirty more were issued to the 11th Hussars and, fitted with special sand tyres, were used successfully in North Africa, but the thin armour and limited armament meant they quickly became out of date, so were retired in 1942. Even with the extra armour, the front end of the CS9 was distinctly a Morris.

As for kits, Resicast have done a very neat resin model in 1/35 and Bolt Action have a 1/56 (28mm wargames scale). For the small-scale modeller, the CS9 has been available in 1/76 scale as a resin kit from Milicast; there are also metal models available from other manufacturers.

Rolls-Royce

One of the best-known British armoured cars must be the Rolls-Royce. Way back in 1914, the War Office acquired all available chassis of the Rolls-Royce Silver Ghost car, and had an armoured body fitted to 120 of them. They carried an enclosed turret mounting a Vickers machine gun. As the war on the Western Front bogged down in the trenches, there was little opportunity to make use of the new armoured cars so many were sent to the Middle East, where they served in Palestine, Egypt and Iraq. Used in combat against the Turks, the Rolls-Royces were famously used by Lawrence in his support of the Arab Revolt.

After World War I, a few were given to the Irish Free State government for use in the Irish Civil War (1922–3) against the IRA, where they were especially useful for convoy escort duties. That still wasn't the end of their story, though, as many remained in the Middle East. They had some modifications in 1920 and again in 1924. There were seventy-six still in service by the time World War II broke out, and they were again used for patrol, escort and reconnaissance work. One modification at this time was the fitting of a new open-top turret to thirty-four examples in Egypt, armed with a Boys anti-tank rifle and Bren LMG plus a smoke grenade launcher. The 11th Hussars operated them in the Western Desert until they

A metal model of the Morris CS9 in 1/72.

were finally replaced by the end of 1941 as more modern replacements became available. A few were so worn out that the bodies were removed and added to a new Fordson truck chassis, becoming the Fordson Armoured Car, while outwardly still looking like the original Rolls-Royce.

Surviving Rolls-Royce Armoured Cars

The Tank Museum at Bovington regularly use their surviving example of the Rolls-Royce armoured car, driving it in the arena at their regular shows. In 2013, it was accompanied at their Tankfest event by another beautifully restored example, Sliabh na mBan, which belongs to the Irish army. The engine cover on this one was opened up to reveal the condition of the engine, which was simply superb, including some highly polished copper.

Front view of the surviving Rolls Royce from the Irish army museum at the Curragh, a car that reached its 100th birthday in 2020.

A close-up view of the immaculate engine in the Irish Rolls.

Rear view of the Irish car, which has quite a history in itself.

The Tank Museum's own example of the Rolls Royce armoured car, which makes a regular appearance in the arena – in this case at Tankfest in 2010.

Another view of the Tank Museum example, in paler green colour than the Irish example.

As for models, there have been quite a few on the market over the years and in a variety of scales. The most recent is a really lovely 1/35 plastic kit from Meng Models, which comes with options and markings for both World War I and World War II designs. Roden have released both 1/35 and 1/72 kits as well, while there were also resin models available in the past, in 1/35, 1/72 and 1/76 scales.

While preparing this book I did come across a few models in a drawer from some years ago. Reviresco was a US producer that made a number of 1/72 scale metal-cast models of armoured cars, and they included some Rolls-Royce variants. I have four, and these are British Army 1917; 1924 Pattern (different turret); 1924 Pattern Western Desert 1940 (open-top turret); and Rolls-Royce a/c on Fordson Chassis 1940.

A 1/35 resin model of the Rolls-Royce armoured car, built before any plastic alternatives were on the market.

Small-scale Rolls-Royce, a Milicast model with the open-top turret.

Packs from Reviresco with four different Rolls-Royce variants, including the Fordson.

When building metal models, bear in mind that some metals have a lead content, so wear disposable gloves if you can and always wash your hands well after handling.

Daimler Mk I and II

The Daimler armoured car was another BSA design, built around the same time as they were working on the Dingo. Initially this was due to have four-wheel steering as well, but experience from the Dingo led to them deciding to stick with standard front-wheel steering only. Essentially it was a slightly larger version of the Dingo, with similar advanced features in the drivetrain. This one didn't enter service, though, until 1941, when the first ones saw action in North Africa, then Italy and Northwest Europe, only a small number making their way to the Far East.

This one, unlike the Dingo, mounted an enclosed turret, armed with a 2-pounder main gun and roof-top hatch cover. The turret may look familiar to tank enthusiasts, as it is the same as the one used on the Tetrarch Light Tank. The 2-pounder was sometimes fitted with an extension to the gun barrel, known as the Littlejohn Adapter, which was essentially a squeeze gun bore adapter to give the round a higher velocity, and thus more hitting power, against heavier German armour as the war progressed. It was another popular and reliable car that went on to serve in various countries around the world long after World War II was over. Built in two marks, just short of 2,700 armoured cars were produced by 1945.

In addition, there were one or two field modifications to create a command car, where the turret was simply removed. These became known as the SODs (Sawn Off Daimlers).

Inside the Daimler Armoured Car

The Daimler armoured car shown here was pictured at War and Peace Revival in 2008. The photos serve to illustrate that the interior of British-built and enclosed armoured cars had a basic silver/aluminium colour, which helped keep the interior light for the crew when the hatches were closed up.

The Daimler armoured car.

The open crew access hatch on the lower right-hand side.

Looking inside and up into the rear of the turret.

Looking up into the forward driver's position and the hinges for his visor; part of the turret ring is in view on the upper left.

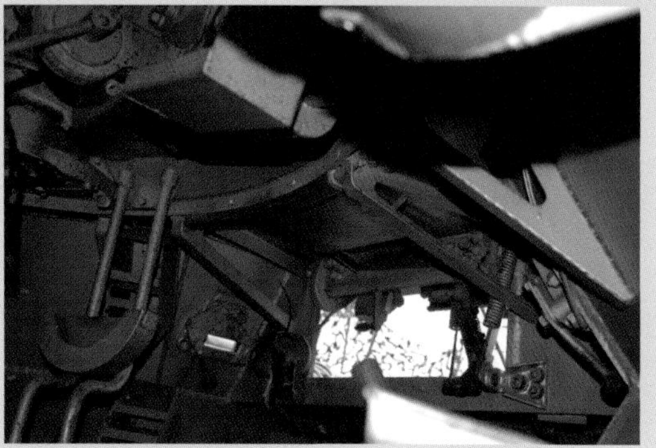

The rear-facing driver's position.

The interior shows the silver/aluminium colour used in British-built AFVs. The tubular supports link the floor of the turret basket to the turret itself, so the crew standing on it turn with the turret.

As for models, the Daimler is still one we are waiting for as a 1/35 plastic kit, though there are resin kits of both the Mk I and the Mk II in the range from Accurate Armour. These are good-quality models, and, with a solid resin hull, there are no internal details to take up your build time.

In smaller scales, Hasegawa did their 1/72 scale kit many years ago, though it was not one of their best in my opinion. My favourites are the good-quality 1/76 metal models from the MMS Models range. There have also been small-scale resin models, particularly from Milicast. Both Milicast and SHQ have done the SOD.

Humber

The most numerous British armoured car of World War II was the Humber. It was made by the Rootes Motor Group, a company that finally went out of business in the 1960s, their brands swallowed up by the Chrysler Corporation. One of the group companies was Karrier, who were building artillery tractors for the Indian army but were really a well-known make at the time. They used the Karrier chassis, added the armoured body from the Guy armoured car and manufactured it under the better-known Humber name.

Box art for the 1/35 resin kit of the Daimler Mk I armoured car.

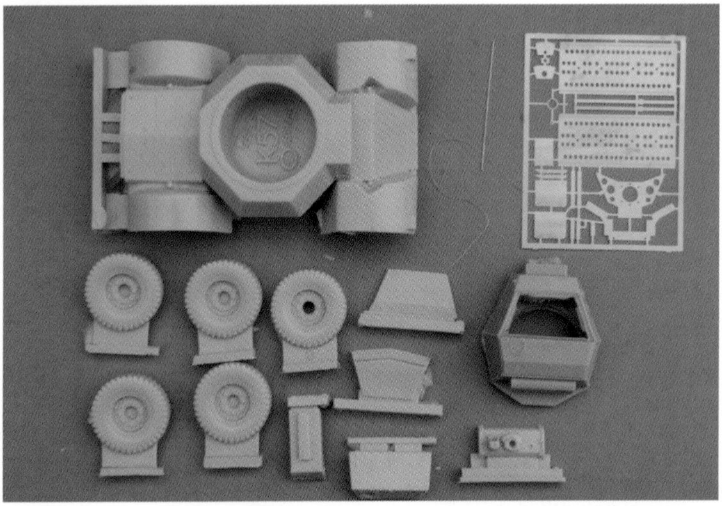

Major parts layout for the Accurate Amour kit.

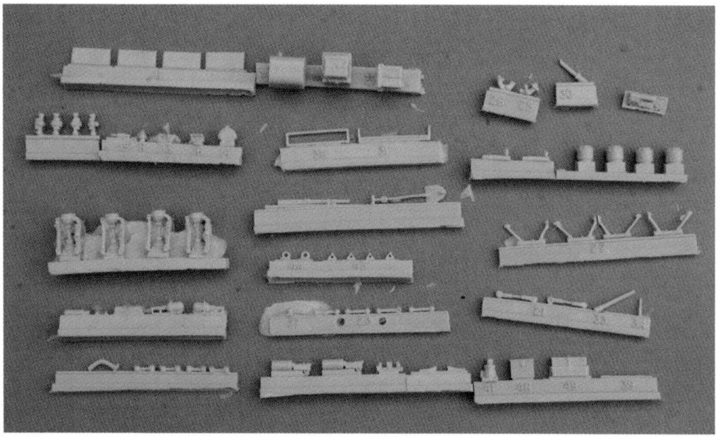

This is the layout of the smaller, detail/fittings parts of the Accurate Armour kit.

A1/76 metal Daimler by MMS Models.

The Daimler SOD, a 1/76 resin model from Milicast. There is a metal version available from SHQ as well.

A Humber armoured car seen at the War and Peace show at Beltring in 2005.

A total of almost 5,500 were built during the war, in marks I to IV:

- The Mk I was essentially the Guy design, armed with a 15mm BESA and a 7.92 BESA machine gun mounted in a turret, and with a three-man crew.
- The Mk II was simply an improved version, eliminating some of the issues with the early Mk I.
- The Mk III introduced a larger turret with room for three, so allowing for the addition of a radio operator and bringing the total crew to four.
- The Mk IV had yet another new turret, improving the armament by fitting a US 37mm M5 gun, but this meant reducing the crew back to three because there was less interior space for a radio operator.

There were a couple of special variants, such as an AA version, the Mk IA, with four 7.92 BESA guns with an AA sight and capable of high elevation. The Mk II had an OP (Observation Post) variant, with turret armament changed to two 7.92 BESA guns. Then the Mk III had a version with a dummy gun so the extra space inside could be used for an additional radio and generator to give a 'rear link'.

With models, we are served quite well for the various marks of Humber. The first I remember was a Mk II, a 1/76 kit by Matchbox, now part of the Revell brand; this was not only a good little kit but, as was common for the old Matchbox range, it came with its own small diorama base. It gets re-released from time to time by Revell so you should be able to find one. Hasegawa then did another Mk II, in 1/72. The turret is badly shaped, unfortunately, so this would not be my choice. Other metal and resin models of the Humber in 1/76 or 1/72 followed over the years, including a Mk III from Milicast. More recently, Tamiya have done a very neat little 1/48 Humber Mk IV, one of a range that seems to be gaining in popularity year by year.

Going up to 1/35, the prize has to go to Bronco Models, who do a number of Humber kits in their range, including a Mk II, a Mk III and a Mk IV. They also do a second version of the Mk IV with full interior detailing and a clear plastic hull so you can see the excellent internal elements. These are very detailed models and give excellent end results.

One marvellous benefit of being a member of MAFVA is that two issues in 2020 have included

Unpainted, this is an original Matchbox Humber kit, in the two-coloured plastic they used to use.

The 1/48 kit of the Humber Mk IV from Tamiya.

a detailed look at all these kits and offered advice on the good or bad points about each one, suggesting any modifications that could improve them and including scale plans of the relevant parts. Among our members we have some real AFV experts, who are happy to share their knowledge with other members. You will find further details in the Appendix.

Staghound Mk I

Now for one of my personal favourites, the Staghound. This was a very successful design, one which many countries around the world operated for many years after the end of World War II. It is also a little unusual for being an American design, technically a Chevrolet T17E1. Built to a joint British/American requirement, it never went into service with the US army, however, as they had decided to standardize on the six-wheel M8, but it was built for the British and Commonwealth forces. The design was worked on in 1942, when a well-equipped armoured car was wanted for service in North Africa, though by the time they were being delivered off the production lines in 1943 they were destined for use in Italy and Northwest Europe.

It was a large 4×4 vehicle, well armoured and armed with a 37mm M6 main armament, quite different to the light machine gun so common in other British types. It was in British service that the T17E was named the Staghound. Weighing in at around 14 tons, it was a heavy armoured car and unusually had two 6-cylinder engines, with an automatic gearbox and linked via a transfer box to the drivetrain. The driver had the facility to select either two- or four-wheel drive as necessary.

Too late for the fighting in North Africa, the Staghound proved troublesome in Italy at first, when the war was bogged down and it was restricted by narrow roads and villages. Once the fighting became more mobile it proved its worth in Northwest Europe, serving in squadron and regimental headquarters units. The basic Staghound Mk I had a crew of five (commander, driver, gunner, loader and hull machine gunner). There was a Mk II that was a field conversion, adding a 3in close support howitzer in place of the 37mm and with the hull machine gun removed, but it's not clear how many of these were built.

The Staghound did offer the chance for other changes. The Mk III used the same hull but was fitted with the 6-pounder armed turret from the Crusader Cruiser tank in an effort to up-gun the vehicle. A couple of hundred of these were built and issued to HQ units in the late stages of the war. Another variant carried an AA turret, mounting twin 0.50cal Browning guns in a Frazer-Nash turret that was adapted from one built for use on British MTBs. A figure of around 1,000 examples is given for production of this T17E2. Another support variant was the T17E3, and this used the basic hull but carried the turret of the M8 75mm HMC (Howitzer Motor Carriage). It was trialled but didn't go into production.

One other variation was adapted late in the war, when spare cars were adapted as command cars for senior officers in some units, with their turrets removed and the extra space used for radios/map

A Staghound at War and Peace in 2005; you can clearly see how large these armoured cars are.

tables. Others had experimental fitting for rocket launchers either side of the turret, just as they did with some Sherman tanks.

There are a number of preserved examples in museums and with private owners, so it's not unusual to see a Staghound or two at shows such as War and Peace.

There have been a good variety of Staghound kits on the market over the years, in both smaller 1/76 and 1/72 scales, along with some larger 1/35

The 1/35 resin model from Accurate Armour.

A 1/35 Eastern European model with resin hull and turret and vac-form plastic mudguards.

kits as well. In all cases, this includes plastic and resin kits, plus in small scale metal ones as well.

In 1/35, the first models I built were resin, one produced by Accurate Armour and another from a producer in eastern Europe that I found several years ago, with resin hull, wheels and turret and vac-formed plasticard mudguards. It was a bit more effort than the Accurate Armour kit but the end result I am still happy with.

For those who prefer plastic kits, Italeri have done some nice kits of the Mk I, the Crusader-turreted Mk III and the AA version as well. More recently, Bronco Models have done a couple more variations, one of which includes the fittings for carrying a pair of short bridging spans. Tamiya have the basic Mk I in their range.

As for the smaller scales, there have been a number over the years, including 1/76 resin models by Milicast, Cromwell Models and others, along with metal ones by SHQ, and, I think, Skytrex many years ago, and plastic by RPM.

Guy Armoured Car

The Guy Armoured Car, also referred to as the 'Tank, Light (Wheeled) Mk I', was designed in 1938 and produced in small numbers (101) between 1939 and 1940. The Guy company couldn't manage to build many, as they were occupied making artillery tractors and trucks. It was passed to the Rootes Group, where the hull formed the basis for the more numerous Humber armoured car series (*see* above). The hull was notable for being the first to use welded construction rather than riveted (as the original specification stated), making production quicker and easier. The centrally mounted turret carried a pair of machine guns, either Vickers or BESA weapons. Six examples were in service with the BEF in France 1940 and lost prior to the Dunkirk evacuation.

I only know of the one model of the Guy, and it is a 1/76 resin kit from Milicast in Glasgow. It's easy enough to build and a good choice if you want to add a rarer type of car to your collection.

A Bronco kit of the Staghound, complete with assault bridges.

A 1/76 resin Staghound by Cromwell Models.

The Guy armoured car, a 1/76 model by Glasgow-based Milicast.

AEC Armoured Car

AEC (Associated Equipment Company) was a bus and truck manufacturer who in World War II were already producing their successful Matador gun tractor. The company wanted to develop an armoured car based on the same chassis and built it as a private venture, then presented it to the War Office, who liked it. It was intended to be a wheeled vehicle, but with the protection of a tank of the period. The Mk I (129 built) was fitted with a Valentine tank turret, armed with a 2-pounder. The Mk II had a new turret and carried the more powerful QF 6-pounder, while the Mk III was armed with a QF 75mm weapon. There was an AA version, fitted with a Crusader AA turret, but it didn't go into production. A total of 629 AEC armoured cars of all types were made. The Mk I saw action in North Africa, while Mks II and III were used in Northwest Europe and served on after the war as well.

I have seen a couple of surviving examples on public display, one at the Tank Museum, Bovington, and the other in the Bastogne Barracks collection in Belgium. When you see one of these up close it is quite striking just how big they are. Unlike some armoured cars, the AEC looks tough enough to warrant the description of a 'wheeled tank'.

As for models, there have been a few available over the years. There are small-scale models in 1/76 and 1/72, in resin or metal, while in 1/35 the plastic kits from MiniArt are excellent. They have done kits for each of the Mk I, II, and III.

Box art for the MiniArt 1/35 kit of the AEC Mk II armoured car.

An AEC Mk I resin kit in 1/76. The Mk I mounted the same turret as the Valentine tank.

AEC Mk I Gun Carrier – the Deacon

The Deacon was based on the chassis of the AEC Matador gun tractor. With an armoured half-cab it carried a 6-pounder mounted in an open-backed armoured shield that looked very much like a naval gun turret. Developed in 1942, Deacons were only used in North Africa to meet a requirement for better mobility for the QF 6-pounder anti-tank gun and providing protection for its crew.

Weighing in at just over 12 tons, it had a 4×4 configuration and a crew of four. Of the 175 built, a few were converted to ammunition carriers by removing the gun. Once the North African campaign ended in 1943, they were all retired as they were not felt to be suitable for combat in Europe.

I have a fondness for the Deacon, though at the moment there's still only one in my collection. I scratch-built mine, using an Airfix Matador kit chassis, one of the first I ever did, based on scale plans in *Airfix* magazine in the late 1960s. I was only about twelve years old when I built it, and this was many years before the internet appeared. As where we lived I couldn't buy plasticard locally, I needed to find a way to build it. I had to make do with what I had on hand; fortunately, it was all flat plates with no awkward curves. My solution? I cut the parts based on the drawings using blank postcards. I haven't seen a plain postcard for years, as most of us use email these days, but then they were readily available, and you didn't need a specialist model shop to buy them from. The other kit part I used was the gun itself, which was taken for an Airfix Bren Carrier kit. The detail on mine is not great but at least it looks like a Deacon, and for a first project for a twelve-year-old I am still pleased to have it over fifty years later. However your modelling skills develop, I think it is good to remember where you came from.

More recently, there has been a 1/76 scale resin model released by Milicast Models from Glasgow. They have also done the ammunition carrier as well. If you prefer the larger scale, then look out for the larger 1/35 scale model by Accurate Armour, also a polyurethane resin model. Theirs is out of production at the time of writing but if you are interested, do let them know.

Now over fifty years old, my first scratch-built model, the Deacon.

AEC Dorchester ACV (Armoured Command Vehicle)

Another variant on the Matador chassis was the Dorchester ACV, officially known as the AEC 4x4 ACV. The Dorchester went into production in 1941 and was first deployed to North Africa. At least three examples were captured by the Afrika Korps and two of them were put to use by Rommel, who had them named Max and Moritz. Over 400 Dorchesters were built in total, and a 6x6 version (with a longer nose) was developed late on in the war and continued in service well beyond 1945. There is a surviving example on display in the Land Warfare hall at IWM Duxford, Cambridgeshire.

As for models, this is another one with all flat plates, so again I was able to scratch-build it on the Airfix Matador chassis. There is little need to do it yourself these days, however. The closest you might want to get to it is a beautifully detailed conversion that uses a lot of etch brass (and the Airfix Matador chassis), which is available from Dan Taylor Modelworks.

If you are a fan of 1/35 then you can have a real treat, thanks to manufacturer AFV Club. They do two variations on their kits, one with British colours and markings and the other with the German fittings and Max or Moritz markings to apply over the remaining British Caunter camouflage scheme. With interior detail for the cab and the command body, these really are beautiful models. The German one has details such as German radios and an Enigma coding machine among the fittings to go inside the bodywork.

The Dorchester also offers an opportunity to include a slightly different option for Braille scale fans. There are a number of reasons why people who like military vehicle models are unable to build and paint their own – maybe advancing age or disability. These enthusiasts might be interested

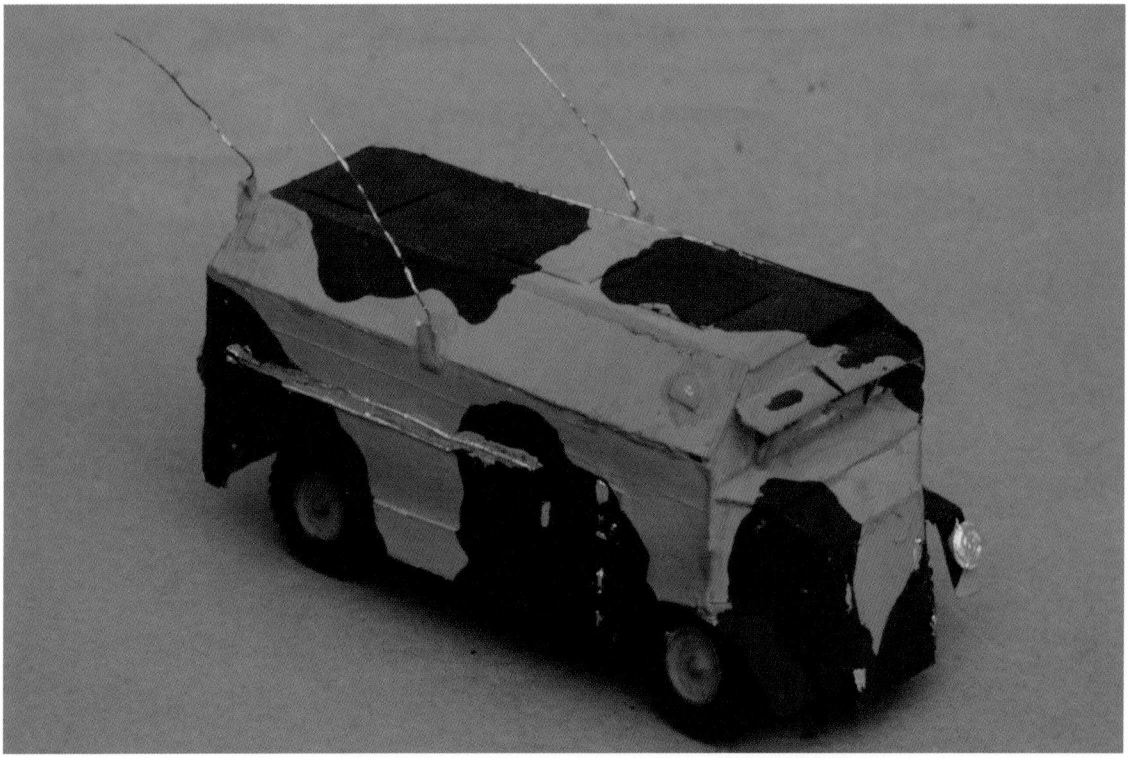

A Dorchester, another of my early attempts at scratch-building, now over fifty years old.

The superb 1/35 kit of the Dorchester from AFV Club.

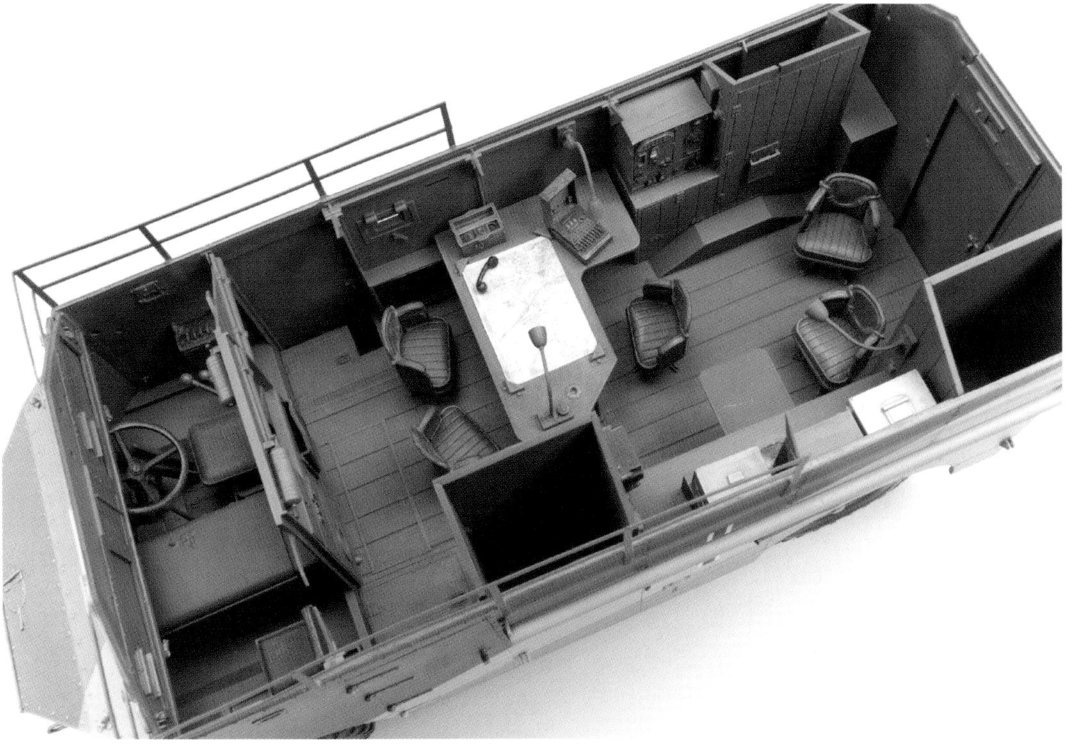

The detailed interior of the Dorchester, with German radios and coding equipment, from AFV Club.

Ready-built Dorchester models from Oxford Diecasts, showing two optional colour and marking schemes.

in a range of diecast models from Oxford Diecasts. They have a huge range of models, including a military series, and among these are a couple of Dorchesters, one of which is in German markings. This modern generation of diecast models is very well detailed and also reasonably priced. Even modellers who prefer to build and paint their own may like these ready-finished diecast models, while for those with disabilities, they are a great way to build their own collection.

AEC Heavy Cockatrice Flamethrower

According to myth, a cockatrice was a two-legged dragon with a rooster's head. It became reality in 1940 when the Petroleum Warfare department worked on building a simple box-shaped armoured body on an AEC 6×6 chassis (the same as was in use for RAF refuellers and done as a kit by Airfix) and armed it with a flamethrower and a couple of machine guns to create the AEC Heavy Cockatrice. Intended for airfield defence, it didn't go into large-scale production, but six were made. The idea of a flame gun is an obvious link to a dragon and hence the choice of name. Apparently there was also a Light Cockatrice, built on the Bedford QL chassis, and sixty of these were used for airfield defence in the UK.

In 1940, with so much equipment being lost in France by the BEF and the threat of invasion, there was some urgency to creating new weapons in case we were to be invaded by the rampant German army. When you look at the rather Heath-Robinson appearance of the Heavy Cockatrice you can see where this led in the field of weapons development, making do with what was on hand.

One option for the modeller would be to source some scale drawings and build it using the Airfix kit chassis, but thankfully it can be much easier than that: Matador Models has a 1/76 resin model in their range for the Cockatrice. As with any resin model, you need to look over the parts when you take them out of the box and check for any blemishes that may need a bit of filler. It's then best to wash the parts first, to remove any

The Heavy Cockatrice, a 1/76 resin kit from Matador Models.

mould-release agent, and allow them to dry overnight before you start the assembly.

This is easy enough as instructions are included. Use superglue, and, once the model is built, give it a spray coat of primer; I use grey acrylic primer spray cans from Halfords, which is well priced and very easy to obtain. Car accessory shops anywhere would probably stock a similar product.

Once primed, I will use a coat of overall SCC 2 Brown, along with a disruptive pattern of SCC 13 Blue-Black, both of which you can find in the excellent 'British Tanks France-Europe-UK, Set 2' from Lifecolor Paints, available through their UK distributor, The Airbrush Company.

CANADIAN UNITS

Volunteers from Canada rallied to support the UK and France at a time of war. The country also assisted with the motor manufacturing industry, producing the series of CMP (Canadian Military Pattern) trucks. They were built by both Ford and Chevrolet (General Motors). A significant advantage, of course, was that they were way out of range of enemy bombing, so production could carry on without fear of disruption.

As well as a significant contribution by way of vital trucks, there were some useful armoured vehicles on the CMP chassis as well – an armoured truck (CT15TA) and similar-looking armoured car (Otter).

Otter

Officially the 'Car, Light Reconnaissance Mk I', this is essentially similar to the CT15TA, using the same 4×4 chassis, but with a fully enclosed armoured body and topped by a small, open-topped turret, fitted with a Bren LMG, plus a Boys anti-tank rifle mounted in the front of the hull. The Otter had a crew of three – commander, driver and gunner. There were 1,761 built in 1942 and they served with Canadian forces in Italy and Northwest Europe, along with some used by South African units and the RAF Regiment. As with the CT15TA (which was a development from the Otter) there is a privately owned example that is another regular at military vehicle rallies.

CT15TA

The CT15TA was an armoured but open-topped troop carrier, with seating for eight soldiers plus the two-man crew. It had a 4×4 design and was built on the Chevrolet C15 CMP pattern truck, with an armoured body made by the Hamilton Bridge Company. The carriers served with both British and Canadian units in Northwest Europe, and many were left behind at the end of the war, when they helped re-equip countries such as Belgium, the Netherlands, France and others. Some left in the Far East were passed on to French forces in Indochina. A total of 3,961 were built during 1943–4. As a result of being kept in use long after the end of the war, there are a number preserved in museums and in private ownership, so you are likely to find an example or two at events like the annual War and Peace Revival in Kent.

There are kits of both the CT15TA and the Otter available in plastic in both 1/35 and 1/72 scale from the Polish manufacturer, IBG. There is plenty of detail in the kits, including inside the crew compartment, and the sprues do tend to have a lot of sprue attachments; especially with the smaller-scale models, some of the delicate parts need to be very carefully removed from the sprue and cleaned up with a sharp-bladed craft knife. They actually build up rather nicely in the end, and it is good to have kits of this late-war armoured truck readily available.

The 1/72 Otter, complete with interior detailing, by IBG.

Box art of the 1/35 C15TA armoured truck, also from IBG.

CMP Otter and CT15 in Real Life

With the IBG models in mind, shown here are a CMP Otter and CT15 armoured truck at the War and Peace Revival in Kent to give an idea of the interior. Built in Canada, and different from the silver/aluminium finish in British-built machines, the Otters had a white-painted interior, with any colour added by equipment such as packs, rifles, seats, head pads and even the steering wheel.

The left front of a CMP Otter, seen at Beltring in 2008.

Right rear of the Otter, which includes some colour and marking ideas.

Inside the Otter. Note the interior colour is white but the steering wheel black, and the interior face of opening hatches is in the exterior base colour.

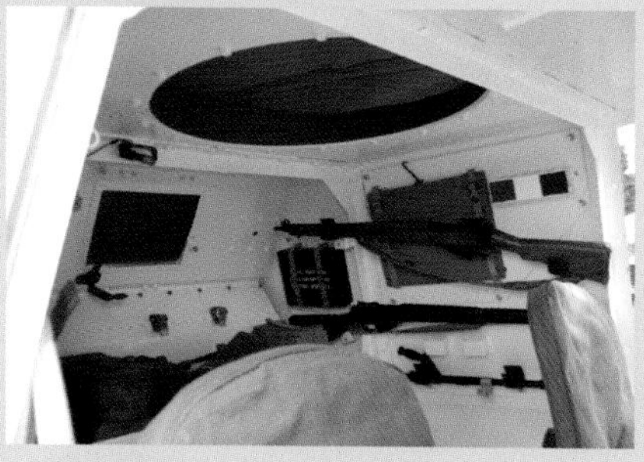

Looking behind the driver's seat, you can see the turret ring in the roof and various stowage items, including a Lee-Enfield No. 4.

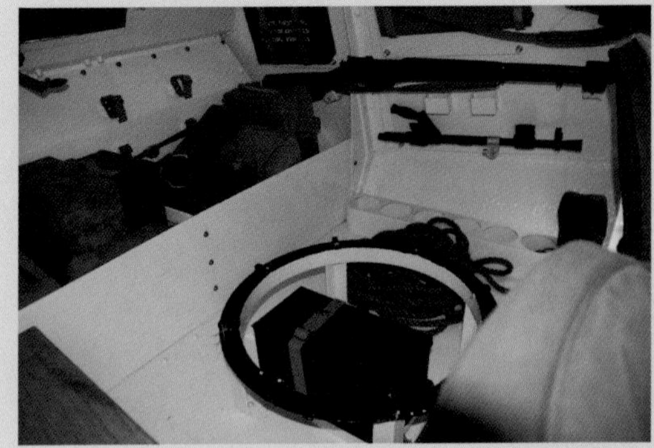

Slightly lower, another stowed Lee-Enfield No. 4 with a spare Bren barrel beneath it and the base for a stand for a crewman to stand on when using the turret.

Looking at the CT15 from the rear, you have a good view of the rear access door and the canvas cover in place over the body. Note the canvas bucket hanging on the back.

Front view of the CT15 armoured truck also seen at the War and Peace show at Beltring, Kent.

The driver's position on the CT15. Note the interior colour for an open-top vehicle is the same as the external camouflage. Also note the wooden steering wheel and the metal case of the fire extinguisher in the foreground.

Fox

The Canadian-built Fox was another to make use of the CMP 4×4 truck chassis. It was fitted with an adaptation of the Humber armoured car body, so they look remarkably similar. On the Fox, the armament was a .50cal Browning with a .30cal alongside it in the turret. It had a crew of four – commander, driver, gunner and radio operator. Foxes were used in Italy and Europe by Polish and Canadian forces, with a few going to India. A total of 1,506 were built and they went on to give good service to other nations, such as Portugal, the Netherlands and later the independent Indonesian army, in some cases right up to the mid-1970s.

Lynx

Such a successful design as the Dingo created a demand for more. Ford in Canada duly started producing the Lynx, using the same Ford flathead V8 engine from the CMP series and with the same

The Ford-built Lynx, a version of the Dingo, as a 1/76 model from Milicast.

A small-scale resin model of the Indian Pattern Carrier.

basic layout as the British-built Dingo, though a little larger overall. Naturally the Lynx was used by Canadian forces in Northwest Europe, having entered service in 1943. Prior to that, the Canadians had used some Dingos during the ill-fated raid on Dieppe in 1942. It was a great pleasure to see a Lynx in the arena at Tankfest a few years ago.

As for models, a good indication of the depth of the Milicast range of 1/76 World War II subjects is the presence of a neat little model of the Lynx in their range.

INDIAN UNITS

Indian Pattern Carrier

With the huge scale of World War II and the loss of equipment in France from the BEF, production capacity in the UK for military equipment, and especially vehicles, was under great strain. Help from other Commonwealth countries was therefore an enormous benefit. They generally lacked the specialized industry that was needed for tanks, but production of lighter armoured vehicles was certainly possible. One answer was the Armoured Carrier, Wheeled, Indian Pattern, which was built onto Ford and Chevrolet 4×4 CMO chassis imported from Canada, with the addition of armoured bodies mostly built by Indian Railways. These carriers were in production from 1940 to 1944, and 4,655 were built. They served largely in Indian army divisional reconnaissance regiments, not only in the Far East, but also in North Africa and the Mediterranean. Armament, like on many other Allied armoured cars, consisted of a Boys anti-tank gun and a Bren LMG. There were a few variants, the bulk of which all had an open-top hull, though some were built with a roof and small turret, not unlike the Canadian Otter.

As for models, I have only ever seen small-scale examples. There was a 1/76 metal model from one manufacturer who is sadly no longer with us, C.A. 'Tommy' Atkins, who cast them in pewter. More recently, Milicast has released two new resin versions, one with bolted and the other with welded armour hulls. I know there are models available in other scales, such as 1/100 from Flames of War, a wargames series, along with a 1/35 kit of the Mk II done by IMA (International Models Asia).

SOUTH AFRICAN UNITS

South Africa, part of the Commonwealth, was another country quick to support the UK in a time of war. Once again, their factories were way out of range from enemy attack, so production lines were free to work undisturbed. At the outset, the country did not have a well-established AFV manufacturing industry, so it relied on imported components such as a chassis from Ford Canada and a drivetrain from Marmon-Herrington in the USA, while it used the armour plate made by the South African Iron & Steel Industrial Corporation.

Marmon-Herrington Armoured Cars

There were four marks of Marmon-Herringtons. The Mk I was a four-wheel car but with only rear-wheel drive; it was used in North Africa at a time when the shortage of equipment meant that if something was available, then it would be useful. Some 113 of these were built before the Mk II introduced a four-wheel-drive version with a slightly longer chassis. It was also fitted with a turret and a slightly improved armament: rather than the two Vickers MGs of the Mk I, the Mk II had a Boys anti-tank rifle plus a Vickers or Bren MG. Production of this version climbed to 887, with the earlier versions using riveted construction and the later ones welded. The Mk III, with a slightly shorter chassis and one or two other changes in the bodywork, made up the bulk of the production run, with over 2,600 built. The Mk IV still used the basic components but in a major redesign and with a QF 2-pounder gun in the turret. Over 2,000 of these were built as well.

The later variants came towards the end of the North African campaign and were not found to be suitable in Italy so were not used much more, though a fair number ended up in the Far East with the Dutch East Indies Army and some stayed in the Middle East after the war, where they were used in Transjordan.

One other thing to add about the Marmon-Herrington in North Africa was that a good number were converted by workshops, having their turrets removed to allow for the fitting of more powerful armament thanks largely to both German and Italian weapons that were captured during the fighting. These included various Breda guns, along with the 3.7cm Pak 36 and the unusual 2.8cm sPzB 41 squeeze-bore anti-tank gun.

For the modeller there have been a good selection of kits available over the years, including small-scale resin and metal models in 1/76 scale from various manufacturers such as SHQ, MMS, Milicast, Giesbers Models and (in plastic) Attack Models. Then, in larger 1/35 scale, there are plastic kits of different marks by IBG and in resin from IMA.

An MMS 1/76 metal model of a Marmon-Herrington with the turret replaced with an Italian Breda Model 35 20mm dual-purpose gun.

Marmon-Herrington Mk VI

Though it never went into service, it is also worth including the Marmon-Herrington Mk VI. Only two prototypes were built, both of which survive, one in South Africa and the other at the Tank Museum, Bovington. It is especially interesting for being an 8×8 design, heavily influenced by the successful deployment of eight-wheel cars by the Wehrmacht. The Mk VIs had an open-topped turret; one of the two (now in the South African Military Museum) mounted a 6-pounder gun, and the other (now at Bovington) a 2-pounder.

Unfortunately, the trials didn't mirror the capabilities of the German eight-wheelers so the project never went any further, but it does remain an interesting part of the Allied armoured car story. The good news is that there is also a small-scale resin model available thanks to Dutch firm Giesbers Models. This is a neat and simple model that will add an unusual machine to any collection.

The Giesbers model of the Marmon-Herrington Mk VI.

The surviving Marmon-Herrington prototype on display at the Tank Museum, Bovington.

Gecko Models have announced they are going to release a new 1/35 plastic kit of the Daimler Mk I armoured car, including internal detail, in 2021.

Chapter Three

German and Axis Armoured Cars

KUGELPANZER

There are plenty of armoured cars to cover here but I thought I'd start with something of an oddity that might or might not be considered an armoured car: the Kugelpanzer. This strange-looking machine has no track but a round, ball-shaped hull only big enough for a one-man crew. The rounded sides are effectively wheels, and a small rear stabilizer makes it a three-wheel armoured reconnaissance vehicle.

The Kugelpanzer was built only as prototype examples, which were sent to Japan for use in the Far East; at least one was captured by the Russians and that now survives in the collection at Kubinka. There are recent models, in 1/35 from Das Werk (with two in the box) and Russian copies from MiniArt, while Attack Models do a small but neatly detailed resin model in 1/72.

From Attack Models, a 1/72 resin model of the odd-looking Kugelpanzer.

GERMAN FOUR-WHEEL TYPES

Kfz 13 and 14

The earliest armoured cars of the Nazi regime were simple, 4×2 vehicles based on the Adler Standard 6 Kublesitzer (bucket-seater) passenger car, and these used what was essentially a civilian car chassis with a lightly armoured open-top body plus a pintle-mounted machine gun, giving the new Wehrmacht the Kfz 13 (Kfz being short for *Kraftfahrzeug*, motor vehicle). There was also another version, fitted with a radio and identifiable by having a fixed-frame aerial fitted around the crew compartment. This was the Kfz 14. It was not a great design but it worked and provided a valuable training tool with which the new Wehrmacht could practise/perfect their skills. As it was, these armoured cars were still used in combat at the outset of the war, in Poland, France and the Balkans, and possibly even in the early stages of Operation *Barbarossa*, the invasion of Russia in 1941.

There are kits of both Kfz 13 and 14 available in small scale. MMS did lovely metal models of both types in 1/76 scale that were nicely detailed and easy enough to build. If you are lucky you might find the odd one for sale on eBay or on a bring-and-buy stand at a model club event.

There is also a 1/72 scale kit available for the Kfz 13 from S-Model, and these have the advantage of not only being excellent little models but including two complete kits in the box. Alternatives can

Two plastic Kfz 13 kits from S-Model and another one plus the radio-equipped Kfz 14 in metal by MMS.

also be found in the First to Fight series. Only one kit in the box this time, but they do come with a magazine that provides more of the history of the type. These are nice, simple models to build that go together well and look good.

For those who like the larger scale, both the Kfz 13 and 14 are in the Bronco range. Bronco has a good reputation for highly detailed models, as we will see shortly, so these will be good kits to go for.

One thing to add about these is that they are largely painted in overall Panzer Grey, though in fact some would have worn a pre-war camouflage with a brown disruptive pattern.

Sdkfz 221/2/3 series

After the early Adler series, which was very much an interim solution, the Heereswaffenamt (Army Weapons Agency) worked in the mid- to late 1930s to develop new military vehicle designs, rather than simply making use of existing civilian products. They had the admirable aim of wanting to create standard (*Einheits*) designs that were intended to ease manufacture and servicing. There was a list of requirements, which included things such as an ability to use various fuel grades, a good cross-country capability, high ground clearance, good turning circle and more. This led to the Standard Chassis for the Heavy Car. Chassis 1 had a rear-mounted engine, intended for armoured cars, while Chassis 2 had a front-mounted engine, and this was the one used for unarmoured field cars (such as the Horsch). The rear-mounted engine chassis became the basis of the Leichter Panzerspähwagen (light reconnaissance car), the Sdkfz 221 series. This included:

1. Leichter Panzerspähwagen (MG) Sdkfz 221
2. Leichter Panzerspähwagen Sdkfz 221 with 2.8cm sPzB 41
3. Leichter Panzerspähwagen Sdkfz 221 with PzB 39
4. Leichter Panzerspähwagen Sdkfz 222 (2cm)
5. Leichter Panzerspähwagen Sdkfz 223 (Fu)
6. Kleiner Panzerfunkwagen Sdkfz 260
7. Kleiner Panzerfunkwagen Sdkfz 261

The most common were 1, 4 and 5, with the others only being built in small numbers. One point to note about the early Sdkfz 221 was that it wasn't equipped with a radio – communication was limited to semaphore flags. Production was ended in 1942 but many served on through to the end in 1945. They were used on all fronts, including in North Africa.

There have been a lot of models of these small armoured cars over the years, in a range of scales. As I have mentioned before, a clockwork-powered model of the 222 was one of my earliest larger-scale kits. In plastic, Airfix did one in a Reconnaissance set but this has never been in my list of favourites as it lacks the anti-grenade screens that are so distinctive on the turret. There was also an early Fujimi kit (in 1/76) that I still like. This has the turret top screens, even though they are in solid plastic.

More recent kits from Dragon, First to Fight and ICM are much better small-scale versions. ICM, though perhaps better known for their 1/35 kits, also do the rarer Sdkfz 260 and 261 radio cars, and these are both neat little models. While there have been both resin and metal small-scale models of the Sdkfz 222 series over the years, the availability of the modern plastic kit has reduced the market for them.

There are also 1/35 kits, particularly from Tamiya and, more recently, HobbyBoss, which is strong on interior detail as well. Their Sdkfz 223

This is the unarmed Sdkfz 260, a 1/72 kit by ICM.

Front view of an actual Sdkfz 223 in the collection at Fort Benning, Georgia.

Rear view of the Sdkfz 223 at Fort Benning.

includes not just the chassis but the rear-mounted engine, along with the internal crew compartment fittings.

Building a Dragon 1/72 Sdkfz 223

As a build example I'll take a look at the Sdkfz 223 in 1/72 from Dragon, one of the sets that comes with two complete kits in the box.

I won't describe the build itself as, frankly, that is very straightforward. The fit of parts is good and, with no internal details to the hull, it builds easily and can be done quite quickly. The turret has the MG 34 and there are crew seats. The only things I didn't glue in place at this stage were the etch-brass anti-grenade screens.

Once built, the next thing was to give it a coat of grey primer. Here I have given it a spray coat of Panzer Grey, using the Tank Spray aerosol from The Plastic Soldier Company, which is great for a basic, single-colour coat. It is easy to use and goes on perfectly and, unlike an airbrush at this stage, doesn't then need cleaning out. Then the two seats in the turret are brush painted in a brown leather and the MG 34 is a matt black (I use Vallejo for this). I used to use gunmetal but have found I prefer black as my standard finish, with, if appropriate, some gunmetal pigment brushed on. The tyres are also painted at this stage, and for these I use either Dirty Black or Tyre Black from the very useful 'Blacks' set of Lifecolor acrylic paints. Just make sure the paint is stirred well before brush painting.

Box art for the Dragon Sdkfz 223; this one is unusual for having two kits in the box.

The running gear fitted to the lower hull of the Sdkfz 223.

The next job for this one will be to add a coat of Gelbbraun (yellow-brown), the darker sand colour used by the DAK (Deutsches Afrika Korps) in North Africa. Their vehicles were Panzer Grey but were overpainted with the sand colour when they were sent to North Africa. However, that colour was hurriedly applied and wore badly, especially once exposed to the hot temperature and abrasive sand inevitable with desert deployment. In a similar way, winter white camouflage was also applied over the main paint scheme and would quickly become worn. The white paste was temporary, sometimes diluted with water, so wore off easily through rain and simply from the crew climbing in

The built but unpainted Sdkfz 223 from the Dragon kit.

The built Dragon Sdkfz 223, rear view.

The 223 is painted in Panzer Grey and the etch-brass grenade screens beside it are ready to be fitted to the turret.

and out. A more permanent finish was obtained using petrol but, as supplies were more hard to come by, this was less common.

This stage can be brush painted, using an acrylic Gelbbraun colour, available from a number of different manufacturers. In this instance I have experimented and used one by Scalecolor, from their set of German Camo Colours. I have mixed it with an additive from AK Interactive that, once dry, will allow me to remove part of it with a damp cotton bud, letting some of the Panzer Grey base colour show through. This will create a worn effect, as so often seen on Africa Korps vehicles.

For a winter white, an alternative is to use the Aqua Line Winter White Camo colour from Wilder Paints (available in the UK via The Airbrush Company). Paint this on straight from the jar, over the top of the basic colour. Once it is dry, use a wet/damp cotton bud to remove the excess; how much you leave or remove will depend on how worn you want the effect to be. One advantage of this is that if you remove too much you can simply repeat the process until you get it how you want. This can be used on Allied units for the winter period of 1944–5 as well as German vehicles.

Once dry, use cotton buds dipped in water to gently rub away at the areas where you want to show the wear that lets the dark-grey base coat show through. This is usually on the edges and where the crew members would have regularly climbed in and out of the vehicle. It's a good idea to look at some

The Dragon kit painted in basic Panzer Grey.

AK Washable Agent, for use with any acrylic paint.

The grey model was brush painted with an Afrika Korps sand colour (from Scale 75 in this case), which had the AK Washable Agent added.

Let the colour dry, then, using damp cotton buds, rub away the paint where it would have worn, such as on edges and where the crew might climb on the vehicle. You can do something similar with a white snow camouflage too.

reference photos of vehicles in North Africa – or on the Eastern Front, in the case of winter white – to get an idea of how much or how little you want to do. Other details, such as the MG 34 in the turret, the tyres and so on, are then brush painted as well, just leaving the transfers to be applied.

For this, you will need to prepare a couple of things. First, cut out the transfer options you want to use from the sheet supplied in the kit. These are done in individual items or just a couple of items at a time. You also need a pot of warm (not too hot) water to soak them in, some setting solutions (again, there are various options but these days I use the Ammo of Mig Jimenez Decal Set 1 and Decal Fix 2), plus a pair of tweezers and some cotton buds.

Put the decal you want to apply into the water to soak through and, meanwhile, using the brush in the bottle, apply the Decal Set solution to the spot on the model where you want to position it. Then remove the decal from the water and, to check it has released correctly, see if you can move it on the backing sheet. Move it to the edge of the backing paper, then use the tweezers to hold it and position it on the model. Once it is in place and positioned correctly, use a cotton bud (or a soft cloth) to press it down carefully into place, pushing out any water and air from beneath it so it grips the surface. Then use the brush from the fixing solution to apply that on top, gently repeating the process with the cotton bud/cloth to remove any excess. Repeat this process for all the decals.

Box art for the well-detailed HobbyBoss 1/35 Sdkfz 222 kit.

Armoured Kubelwagen

The German military made widespread use of the VW Kubelwagen, a small utility vehicle that is roughly equivalent to the US Jeep. It was just a two-wheel drive but used on every front during World War II. Only built in small numbers, the lightly armoured version, which carried an MG 34 mounted in a turret on the solid roof, had bulletproof glass and bulletproof tyres filled with sand. Between eighty and a hundred were built and they served mostly on the Eastern Front.

I have one resin model of the little armoured Kubelwagen in my collection, a resin model in 1/76, from Cromwell Models many years ago. The main body was a solid resin piece so the question was what to do with the windows. My answer for this was not to use paint but a soft pencil on top of the base coat of paint. This gives a suitable dark-grey colour and the graphite also has a natural sheen to it, imitating the shine of the glass in a quick and simple solution.

Sdkfz 254

This is a really unusual Austrian design, the Saurer RR7/2. A strange-looking machine, it had both tracks and wheels – the RR designation stood for Räder/Raupen (wheels/tracks) – and served as an armoured observation post. Around 140 were built between 1937 and 1939, and once the Anschluss happened in 1938, they were taken into service with

An old Cromwell Models 1/76 resin model of an armoured Kubelwagen. The solid cast windows are coloured simply with a pencil.

The unusual-looking Sdkfz 254, an Austrian built wheel-cum-track machine.

the Wehrmacht, designated as the Sdkfz 254. The tracks gave it a fair cross-country performance and the wheels were for running on roads, which meant extra speed and less wear on the tracks themselves. The wheels used a mechanical arrangement to be raised/lowered to change from one mode to the other, rather than this being a manual task.

There are models available for this rather odd machine. The first I remember, many years ago now, was a resin kit in 1/76, but since then there have been others, including another small-scale one in metal and, in the last few years, a 1/35 plastic one from HobbyBoss. It may be only small but stands out in any collection of World War II armoured vehicles thanks to the wheel-cum-track arrangement of the running gear.

4-Rad Spähwagen 'Neue Art'

This covers just a single example, which was built as a prototype. Apparently it was a Büssing-Nag-built vehicle using the hull of an Sdkfz 234 Puma, but with only four wheels rather than eight (*Rad* meaning wheel). I haven't seen any record of a turret having been fitted, but Ironside Models, a brand from French manufacturer Azimut, released a 1/35 resin conversion for the Italeri Puma kit with the four-wheel hull mounting the 5cm-armed Puma turret. Whether that would actually have been fitted or the 2cm Hangelafette six-sided turret can only be guessed. I built this kit many years ago and finished it in a purely theoretical scheme of camouflage and markings.

This 1/35 Spähwagen is a conversion kit from Azimut Productions.

Sdkfz 247 Ausf B

This one is a 4×4 design, used as a radio/command vehicle but only built in small numbers. Confusion can arise, though, as this is another instance where the same Sdkfz number (247) was also applied to a different model – the Ausf A that had been built on the six-wheel Krupp Kfz.69 chassis (*see* below). For modellers, the good news is that while there was an old resin model in 1/35 by Sovereign 2000, at the time of writing ICM have just released one as a plastic kit. Going by their existing range, this is set to be a good kit to look out for.

Skoda PA-II Zelva (Turtle)

One of the oddest looking armoured cars used in World War II, the Skoda 'Turtle' had been built in the mid-1920s in Czechoslovakia. Technically

Box art for the recently announced Sdkfz 247 Ausf B from ICM.

Box art for the strange, rounded shape of the Skoda Turtle armoured car.

it was the Obrněný Automobil model 1923 (OA vz.23), and was never officially called the Turtle. The curved bodywork all had to be shaped by hand and then riveted to a steel frame. Armament consisted of four machine guns, and they had a crew of five: the commander, two gunners and two drivers so it could be driven either forwards or backwards – though when you look at it, it's difficult to tell which is the front and which is the back.

The Turtle was a four-wheel-drive machine but, while it had a respectable road speed, the cross-country performance was unsatisfactory. The ten built were actually rejected by the Czech army, but once the Wehrmacht acquired them in 1939 they were put to use despite their limitations and stayed in use throughout the war.

I have never felt the urge to build a model of the Turtle but they are available. Pick of the bunch I suspect for many will be the 1/35 kit by Takom. Takom are a relative newcomer to the list of major plastic kit manufacturers of armour models, but they have quickly made an excellent reputation for themselves, so this is likely to be a nice one to build.

SIX-WHEEL TYPES

Sdkfz 231

Now let's move on to the six-wheelers used by the Wehrmacht, particularly in the first half of the war. There are effectively three different types.

The first of these is the Sdkfz 231 series. This in itself can lead to confusion because the designation is the same as that used for the eight-wheeler series. The difference is usually indicated by referencing them as Sdkfz 231 (6-Rad) for the six-wheel, or 8-Rad for the eight-wheelers (*see* below).

Again, the six-wheelers were something of an intermediate design to get something in service quickly and cheaply. They had an armoured hull and turret based on a commercial truck chassis with a front-mounted engine. The only significant difference was that the steering position was duplicated front and rear so it could be driven in either direction, thanks largely to the addition of a new direction-change gearbox that enabled them to be driven in either direction. With single-wheeled, unpowered front axles and twin-tyred rear axles, it must have been a strange experience to have driven these backwards, and I would guess that it didn't happen all that often in practice.

Built by different manufacturers such as Daimler-Benz, Magirus and Büssing-Nag, there were two basic versions. One was a simple reconnaissance car (Waffenwagen) and the other was essentially the same, but fitted with a large frame aerial for the more powerful radios they were fitted with (Funkwagen). The basic car was designated the Sdkfz 231, while Sdkfz 232 indicated the version fitted with a 100W long-range wireless. Both were armed with a 2cm KwK 30 or 38 cannon, plus a 7.62 MG 34. The loaded weight of these vehicles was a little over 6 tons. There was also a third version, with a fixed turret, the Sdkfz 263, which was a command variant (Panzerfunkwagen). The frame aerial on this one was a slightly different pattern to that on the 232.

Outwardly each one looks the same, but underneath, each manufacturer used their own commercial lorry chassis/engine, which must have made the spares/maintenance tasks a real problem for the units that operated them. All had front-mounted engines and a 6×4 design, with single front wheels and the two rear drive axles both carrying twin wheels.

Getting on in years, this is an original Matchbox kit of the Sdkfz 231.

First to Fight 1/72 model of the Sdkfz 232.

Finished in the overall Panzer Grey used during the early stages of the war, these saw service in Poland, the Low Countries and France as well as the early stages of the war against Russia and in the Balkans.

As for kits of these six-wheelers, I still remember my pleasure when Matchbox released a 1/76 kit, complete with a small diorama base, back in the 1970s. You could build it as either version, so with or without the frame aerial. Only recently there have been new models, this time in 1/72, which have come out in the First to Fight (FtF) model series. Both the original Matchbox kit (which holds up very well for its age) and the new FtF kits are easy enough to build.

Sdkfz 247 Ausf A

The one other six-wheel armoured car to go into limited production was the Sdkfz 247 Ausf A; again, this is the same designation as the later four-wheel Ausf B mentioned above. This was an open-top command vehicle built on the proven chassis of the Krupp L2H 143 1.5ton 6×4 truck (which was also a well-used gun tractor), with a distinctive sloped bonnet over the Krupp Boxer 4-cylinder engine. Just a few were built with armoured bodies to act as command cars. The one thing these didn't have compared to the Sdkfz 231 was any facility for rear steering.

Building a Bronco Sdkfz 247

As for models, I would pick out the excellent 1/35 kit from Bronco Models. It has been on the market for a few years now and is a very well-made and detailed model.

Box art of the Bronco Models Sdkfz 247 Ausf A.

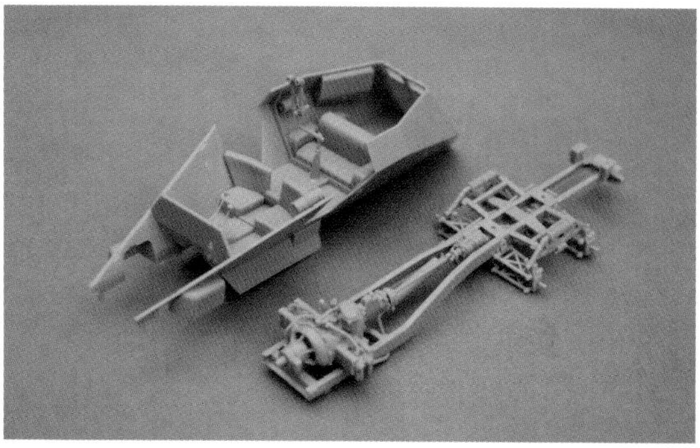

The chassis and powertrain are finished, alongside the lower armoured body, and ready to be joined.

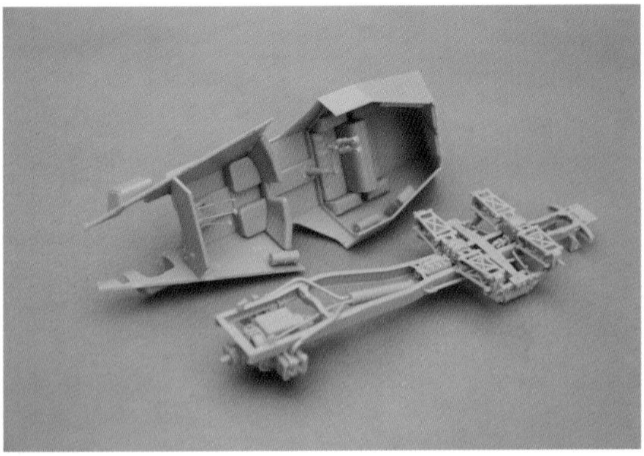

Chassis and bodywork of the Bronco Sdkfz 247 kit during construction.

The breakdown of the chassis and drivetrain alone is relatively complex, with a number of small etch-brass parts involved. For that reason alone I wouldn't suggest it for a beginner, but if you are experienced in building plastic models, then the level of detail in here is an added bonus. My best advice is to take it slowly and just enjoy the build. There are also some really tiny parts, such as the butterfly nuts on the oil filter on the engine, which you need to take off the sprue very carefully as they are so easy to drop and then lose.

The chassis needs to be assembled with the two main beams joined with crossbeams, and it is very important to get everything nice and square or it will cause problems as you fit the running gear. I found one of the crossbeams was slightly out of position on mine once I'd glued it, so that needed to be adjusted. The driveshafts and transfer boxes are also a bit fiddly to fit but are neatly secured once you add the rear suspension arms. The body-work then fits neatly in place and the rest of the assembly is quite straightforward.

For colour and markings, all three options the kit provides for have single-colour Panzer Grey, for which I used the Tank Spray Panzer Grey from The Plastic Soldier Company. This provides a good, even coverage. The seats I brush painted with a Red Leather shade from Lifecolor. The other details to talk about are the pick and shovel, stowed on the outer rear face of the bodywork. Even after all these years, I like to experiment and this time I went for something I'd read about by never tried. For the wooden handles, I used Vallejo Buff paint and then applied some mid-brown grain strips with a very fine brush. At that stage it didn't look brilliant, but the finishing touch was then to paint over them with Tamiya clear orange – giving you what looks like a great varnished wood effect. It was actually quick and simple to do and I am very pleased with the final look.

The plain grey colour was given a coat of Ammo Blue-Grey Filter for Panzer Grey and once that was dry, the simple set of transfers was applied. It was all then sealed with a spray coat of Revell matt varnish and will await some weathering when I decide just what to do with it.

There has also been a 1/72 plastic kit of this one in the First to Fight series.

Built and painted, this is the end result for the Sdkfz 247 Ausf A.

With the 247 painted, the next step is to highlight the detail using a pale grey pigment; again, I have used the Tamiya set.

This view shows how the light grey emphasizes the edges and detail on the model.

Finish with an application of a brown earth-coloured pigment, with emphasis on the lower surfaces.

A Bronco Models 1/35 kit of the Krupp Protze Kfz 69 with armour plates and 3.7cm Pak 36.

Krupp Protze Kfz69 with 3.7cm Pak36

Simple armour plates were added to the Kfz69 Krupp Protze truck and a 3.7cm Pak 36 anti-tank gun was mounted on the rear deck, along with ammunition stowage lockers and seats for more gun crew. Bronco Models makes an interesting 1/35 kit of this strange-looking armoured car that improved mobility for the German Blitzkrieg tactics over the towed version of the gun. It was only built in small numbers, however.

EIGHT-WHEEL TYPES

Magirus M-ARV

I'll start this section by talking about a rare vehicle, the Magirus M-ARV (which stood for Magirus Achtradwagen, or eight-wheel vehicle). It was only built in prototype form in the late 1920s, and actually sent to the then secret testing ground at the Kama Tank School near Kazan in Russia. At this time Germany was still banned from operating armoured vehicles. This was the first of their eight-wheel designs, created to meet a specification for an MTW (Mannschaftstransportwagen, or transport vehicle for personnel). It had a completely new design, rather than being based on any existing chassis, and the uneven spacing of the four axles was a little unusual. It catered for a crew of five. It was also amphibious, with a propeller to be fitted as and when necessary. The centrally mounted turret carried the armament of

The experimental Magirus MATV, a resin kit in 1/72 from Giesbers Models.

two machine guns. Apparently the prototype was eventually returned to Germany, but quite what happened to it after that is unknown.

Having only seen a few photos of this vehicle over the years, I was very pleased to find that Den Bels models in Holland had produced a 1/72 model of the Magirus M-ARV. It's a fairly simple kit, with just some straightforward clean-up to do on the polyurethane resin cast parts; assembly with superglue is quite quick.

Sdkfz 232/234 Series

Next to the obvious choices of the German Panzers, the eight-wheel armoured car series was perhaps one of the best-known armoured vehicle types from World War II. The 232 was built from a requirement issue in 1934 and the design featured an eight-wheel design with eight-wheel drive and all-wheel steering, which also had a driving position at both front and back. These vehicles had a good cross-country capability but were quite a complex design, which would have an effect on both production and then maintenance once in service. As they were intended to take the same roles as the earlier six-wheel cars, they were given the same numerical designation, but used an additional indicator to show which was which. Hence we have already seen the Sdkfz 232 (6-Rad), while this now is the Sdkfz 232 (8-Rad). Obviously there is scope for confusion here, so that extra little bit of information to indicate six or eight wheels is important to remember.

In the first GS series there were four main variants. The first two mirrored the earlier six-wheel series, being the Sdkfz 231 8-Rad Schwerer Panzerspähwagen Waffenträger (weapons vehicle) with a turret-mounted 20mm cannon and MG 34; and the Sdkfz 232 8-Rad Schwerer Panzerspähwagen (Fu) radio vehicle, which had the same turret plus the frame aerial. In addition to these, there were the Sdkfz 233 Schwerer Panzerspähwagen 7.5cm, with the short-barrelled support weapon in an open-top fighting compartment, plus the Sdkfz 263 8-Rad Schwerer Panzerfunkwagen command variant, which had no turret but a higher, fixed superstructure and frame aerial.

A total of 1,235 examples were built across the four variants. They all had a chassis with an armoured hull, and an important recognition point was the two mudguards on either side, each one covering two wheels. Production ended in 1942 but the cars served on through to the end of the war.

Then there is the later Sdkfz 234 series. These vehicles looked largely the same but used the strength of a monocoque hull that supported the running gear, so didn't have the need for a separate chassis.

This new type of eight-wheel car entered production in 1943 and was produced in another four variants. The Sdkfz 234/1, the Schwerer Panzerspähwagen, was fitted with a turret-mounted 2cm gun; Sdkfz 234/2 with a turreted

The quite different chassis of the Sdkfz 234 series on the left and the 232 series on the right.

Two small-scale models of the same basic vehicle: a plastic kit on the left and metal one on the right.

5cm gun (the Puma); Sdkfz 234/3 Schwerer Panzerspähwagen with a 7.5cm Kurz (the short-barrelled support weapon); and the Sdkfz 234/4 Schwerer Panzerspähwagen with 7.5cm Lange, the long-barrelled 7.5cm Pak 40 anti-tank gun, in an open-top fighting compartment.

For all of the 234 series, the major recognition point was the change to a single mudguard on each side, with integral stowage boxes, though there were plenty of other detail changes as well. Another 2,300 of these (across all variants) were built by the end of the war. The other great advantage of the later 234 series was that the new drivetrain arrangements meant the whole vehicle was lower than the previous 231 cars.

As for models, it's hard to know exactly where to start because there are so many. The right one to begin with is probably the old Airfix kit of what they simply called a German Armoured Car, and is essentially an Sdkfz 234/4. It was originally produced in the 1960s but is a bit unfortunate as it mixes the two different series of cars. The armament is the 7.5cm Pak 40, in an open-top fighting compartment, an indicator of the Sdkfz 234 series. However, the hull is fitted with the four mudguards (two each side). Not only do they have sharp edges rather than being rounded as the real ones were, this is also a sign of the earlier Sdkfz 231 8-Rad series, and these weren't fitted with the Pak 40. It should have the full-body-length one-piece mudguards of the Sdkfz 234. When it was released it was the only kid on the block, so it prompted conversion/correction articles in the likes of *Airfix* magazine.

Since then, the availability of kits has blossomed. There are some nice models in 1/100 (15mm) and 1/72 (20mm) scales by The Plastic Soldier Company. With their 15mm scale kit you get five complete models in the box and you can make each one up as you like; with the 20mm kit you get three. These are all for the Sdkfz 231 series, so all with the four distinctive mudguards, and you can make any of the three main variants.

There are also 1/72 kits of the 231 series from First to Fight, a series of relatively simple models from the IBG stable and which come 'free' with the accompanying magazine. More detailed models have been made by Dragon Models. Then there are others in 1/48 from Tamiya, and 1/35 thanks to Italeri and AFV Club. The AFV Club kits are very well detailed, inside and out. I've built their Sdkfz 263, the command variant and it really is a super model, with all the detail on the chassis as well, even though it is hidden away underneath.

The Sdkfz 263 in 1/35 from AFV Club.

As for the 234 series, Hasegawa, Italeri, Roden and Revell (which includes the old Matchbox kit of the Puma) all do 1/72 examples from the series. I know there is also a 1/56 scale from Warlord Games, for use in 28mm scale wargaming, a scale that has grown enormously in popularity over the last few years. Though not a kit I have seen for myself, I am sure this will be neatly done. Bigger still, in 1/35, the Puma and others are available from both Italeri and Dragon Models, all well detailed with the larger turret and long-barrelled 50mm gun.

Building an Sdkfz 232 in 15mm Scale

When it comes to building an example, I thought I'd go small for this one, with the wargamers' 15mm scale, which is the same as 1/100. The kit to go for here is from The Plastic Soldier Company (PSC), which contains five complete models in the box.

A variety of Sdkfz 234 models, including the Italeri 1/35 Puma at the back.

Box art for the 1/35 Dragon kit of the 75mm Pak 40-armed Sdkfz 234.

The Plastic Soldier Company (PSC) kit of the Sdkfz 231 series in 15mm scale.

Sprues for five complete kits in the PSC box.

There are five identical sprues in the box, each one giving you the parts to build any of the four different variants, so you can mix and match what you choose to make up. I'll talk about just one sprue/model, but of course the comments apply equally to all five.

The kit being plastic, it's easy to use sprue cutters to remove the parts from the sprue and then a sharp craft knife to clean off the remaining stubs from the parts where they were connected to the sprue. I use Revell Contacta Professional for most assembly, mainly because I like the thin metal applicator tube that helps be more precise in applying it to the parts. Whichever option you go for, one whole model can easily be assembled in about half an hour or so. There's no need to rush and the fit of parts is spot on. Each sprue is left with a number of unused parts that you can add to your spares box. If you do several kits like this, you will find your spare parts collection soon builds up.

Once built, just decide what colours and markings you want to go for. For many, the plain Panzer Grey is a clear choice. As for markings, there are none provided in the kits themselves, but PSC do a good range of transfers that you can choose from and that offer a lot of individual items in each set.

ADGZ

We come to the end of the eight-wheel armoured cars used by the Germans during World War II with another unusual-looking vehicle, the Austrian Steyr ADGZ, officially known as the M35 Mittlerer Panzerwagen. Built and taken into service from 1934 to 1937, some were used by the Austrian army and others by the police. After the Anschluss of 1938, however, they were taken into German police service, with some going to the Waffen-SS as well. Over fifty were built, including twenty-five additional vehicles that were ordered by the Waffen-SS in 1942.

The ADGZ always puts me in mind of the fictional Pushmepullyou from the Dr Dolittle books by Hugh Lofting, an animal with two heads that can go in either direction. There are of course other armoured cars that can be driven in either direction, but with the ADGZ the design makes it difficult to tell which is the front and which is the back because they both look pretty much the same.

The other oddity is the wheel arrangement. The front and rear axles are both fitted with single wheels, while the two central axles have double wheels, making it a very recognizable armoured car. They weighed in at about 12 tons, were armed

Two variants of the PSC 15mm scale models.

The odd Pushmepullyou arrangement of the ADGZ armoured car, here in the HobbyBoss kit.

In this view you can see the highlighting on the detail, created with Tamiya weathering powders.

with a 2cm KwK cannon and an MG 34 in an enclosed, centrally mounted turret, and had a crew of six. They stayed in service for policing duty to the end of the war, and there is even one in a photo amidst wrecked vehicles in Berlin in 1945.

For models of the ADGZ, there was a 1/76 resin model done a good few years ago by Cromwell Models, while more recently there is a nice 1/35 model in the HobbyBoss range of kits. It is such a strange-looking configuration that it does make for a talking point in any collection.

ITALIAN MODELS

Fiat Spa Autoprotetto S37

Based on the Fiat Spa TS37 gun tractor, there was an armoured troop carrier, the Autoprotetto

An old metal model of the Italian Autoprotetto S37 APC.

An old small-scale resin model of the S37 by US Casts.

S37. Distinctive for the short chassis and the large wheels, it was given an open-topped armoured body. It had no built-in armament, only what the troops had for their personal weapons, although a Breda machine gun was fitted on some. Inside, there were simple bench seats on either side, and the troops had to stand to fight from the vehicle, which left them exposed. A couple of different arrangements were tried to offer them a little more protection. No exact numbers for how many were built are available, but it was something in the region of 200.

Small-scale kits have been done in 1/72, one by Ace Models and another by Reviresco, a metal cast model. There was also once a resin model in 1/76, made by US Casts if I remember correctly.

FIAT Lince

The Italians were impressed by the British Daimler Dingo, so they simply copied it. There were 250 examples built, and they were used by both Italian and German forces in Italy and the Balkans. While it naturally looks very much like a Dingo, a raised central hump on the engine cover is a recognition feature of the FIAT version. Interestingly, they called it the Lince (lynx), which is the same as the name used for the US Ford-built version of the Dingo; presumably this was coincidence, but it's hard to know for sure.

There has been a 1/72 plastic kit done by Ace Models, who produce a series of short-run injection moulded plastic kits, and 1/35 models by Criel and by Maquette as well, but I haven't tried any of these.

Camionetta AS 42 Sahariana

The Sahariana was a low-slung vehicle on the same chassis as the AB-41 with the same rear engine arrangement but with a much lower front end and open-topped crew compartment. It was designed to be a desert patrol vehicle, built as a response to the effectiveness of the LRDG (Long-Range Desert Group) raids on various Italian bases in North Africa. The car was distinctive for having two rows of jerricans stored in racks on either side of the hull, a clear indication of the need to carry both petrol and water supplies for long desert patrols. On later versions, the top row of cans on either side was replaced with stowage boxes.

The Sahariana, in this case a resin model by CMSC with etch-brass detail, for example the sand channels.

The crew compartment was not only open but quite roomy, so there was space for a variety of armament to be fitted from one car to another. Some just had a pintle-mounted machine gun while others carried the 20mm Breda or the Italian 47/32 anti-tank gun, though this was really obsolete by 1942 as it lacked the punch needed for the newer allied tanks. Rather like the British 2-pounder, it was soon outdated. I have not found any firm numbers on how many were built, but it is thought to have been around 100.

There have been a few models of the Sahariana over the years, including 1/72 and 1/35 examples from Italeri. I also have an older 1/76 one from CMSC (Continental Model Supply Company), now gone after the death of the owner. That was a resin kit with metal detail parts. In the larger scale, there have been other 1/35 resin models, such as from Italian model maker Criel, but not one I have seen, unfortunately. A common problem for resin model companies is that once a cheaper, injection-moulded plastic alternative comes on the market, resin kit sales quickly drop.

SPA-Viberti AS 43

A late-war attempt to improve the supply of armoured cars for the Italian armed forces, the AS 43 was based on the TL-37 artillery tractor. It was a front-engined car with a short chassis and was fitted with a turret from the L6/40 light tank. Only a couple were built, so it didn't go into widespread service.

The Italian AS 43.

Fiat Dovunque 33

Based on the Fiat 665 NM, an armoured version of this truck was intended to be an armoured troop carrier. Only a small number were built (fewer than ten), however, and there is one survivor.

I remember that there was a resin kit of this in 1/76 from US Casts, an American producer of resin AFV models but who are no longer in business.

HUNGARIAN MODELS

39M Csaba

This Hungarian armoured car was designed before World War II by Nicholas Straussler, who had been born in Hungary but moved to the UK, where he lived and worked during the interwar period. He worked particularly with Alvis on various armoured vehicles but is perhaps best known for designing the DD (Duplex Drive) system that was used on Sherman tanks for the invasion of Normandy in 1944. Less well known, though, is the fact that he also designed an armoured car for his homeland, and the 39M Csaba went into production for the Hungarian army, named, apparently, after the son of Attila the Hun.

In 1939–40, over 100 were ordered, most being used as command and reconnaissance vehicles. The turret-mounted armament was a 20mm Solothurn anti-tank rifle plus an 8mm machine gun, plus a second, separate machine gun that could be fitted on an AA mount on the rear turret hatch. It had duplicate driving positions, front and rear, a frame aerial around the top of the hull and a total crew of three.

For many years we had little information about the equipment and history of Hungarian armed forces during World War II, but much more has emerged since the collapse of the Warsaw Pact around 1989.

As for models, there are options. For 1/35 scale fans, HobbyBoss have stepped up to the plate with a neat kit of the 39M Csaba, which is quite easy to build. I also have a 1/76 metal model from C.A. ('Tommy') Atkins. Possibly the most awkward

Box art for the HobbyBoss 1/35 Hungarian Csaba.

A built and painted pewter model of the Csaba from C.A. ('Tommy') Atkins, an old range no longer available since Tommy passed away some years ago.

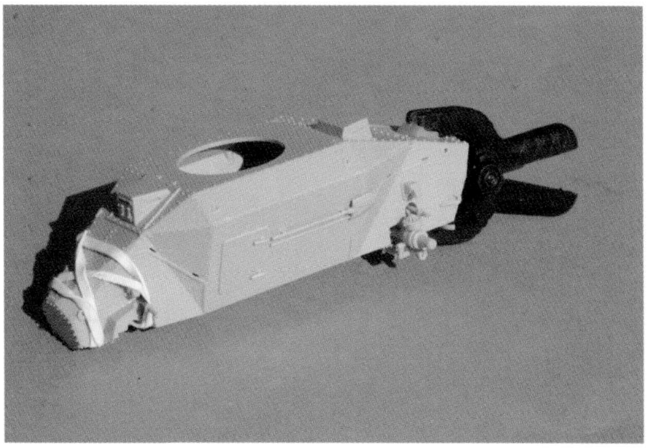

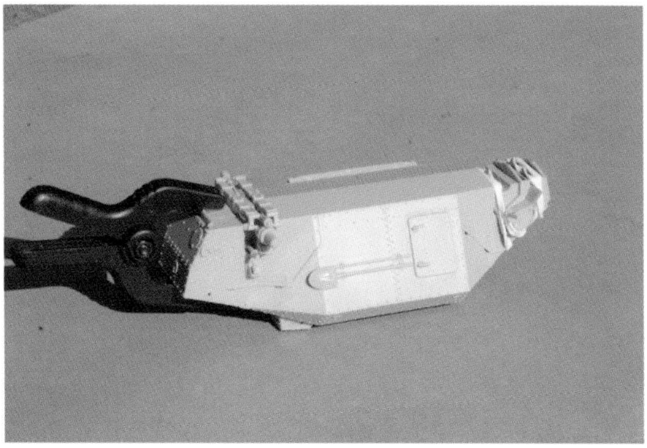

The HobbyBoss 1/35 Csaba under construction. The upper hull was slightly bowed so I used both a clamp and elastic bands to hold the parts together while the bond set.

The HobbyBoss Csaba ready for painting. The wheels won't be fitted until both they and the wheel wells have been painted.

thing to do with these is painting the three-colour camouflage scheme. There is a good colour guide included with the HobbyBoss kit, but whatever the scale, getting the pattern right is not the simplest thing I've ever done.

JAPANESE MODELS

Type 2593 'HoKoKu'

Japan was the other major Axis power, but when we look at the war in the Pacific we don't see much use of armoured cars by either the USA or Japan. There were some used by Commonwealth forces but generally, both in the jungles of Southeast Asia and on the various Pacific islands, the conditions simply didn't make them very useful: there were neither the road networks of Europe nor the clear terrain of North Africa to give them the kind of freedom of movement that characterizes their use.

The one exception, and one that did feature in that old Airfix modelling guidebook, is the Japanese Type 2593 'HoKoKu', also known as the Type 93 'KoKuSan', manufactured by Isuzu. Only a small number were built in the early 1930s and they were used by the Special Naval Landing Force units, especially in the war against China. It had a 6×4 design, and one that could quickly switch between road tyres and rail wheels. Armament was only machine guns, one 7.7mm in the turret plus another four 6.5mm guns in hull mountings. It also had a pair of small auxiliary wheels just behind the front axle, which, like on many armoured car designs, was to help prevent the longer gap between the front and rear axles from grounding and potentially bogging the car down.

As a subject, this one has helped introduce me to the possibilities of 3D printing. For this I have to thank my friend Vincent Mifsud, a fellow MAFVA member. He was kind enough to translate some scale plans into a 3D drawing and print file, so that the model could then be simply printed whenever we want one. In this case he used a plastic filament printer.

Once you have the printed parts, there are some elements to be removed, a bit like sprues on a plastic kit, or casting feed blocks on a resin kit. These usually fill voids, such as under wheel wells and the like. One advantage of this method is that if you do make a mistake and remove the wrong piece, you can just print another. There aren't too many parts to this one, so after the clean-up, check the parts by dry-fitting them and then fix the assembly with superglue. Then you just need to prime and paint.

There are not too many references on these cars, but the best one I know is *Japanese Armor*, Vol. 1 by Andrzej M. Tomczyk, in the TankPower

A computer image of the 3D print file for a Japanese Type 2593.

This is the parts breakdown for the 3D printer. It involves one hull, one turret, one of each of the suspension units and six wheels.

The assembled 3D-printed model.

A Type 2593 3D-printed armoured car assembled and primed.

The book on German camouflage and colours from Ammo by Mig Jimenez.

Series (no. 9) from the Polish publisher AJ Press. It includes colour artwork and scale plans.

Finally, I will conclude this chapter by recommending books on how to apply weathering or a detailed painting guide for German AFVs in particular. The three *Panzer Colours* books by Bruce Culver, published by both Squadron Signal in the USA and Arms & Armour Press here in the UK, are excellent. More recently, another good guide has come from Ammo by Mig Jimenez, not only with some excellent colour profiles but giving help with the sequence in which to apply different weathering effects.

Chapter Four

American Armoured Cars

I still find it a little surprising that the US military in World War II really only used three different armoured cars, plus one other that was more a field modification than a full-blooded armoured car. What is not surprising is that the US motor industry was able to produce them in large numbers, with modern mass-production techniques and no disturbance from enemy action.

ARMOURED JEEP

Let's start with what I'll describe as an extemporized armoured car, as additional armour panels were added to some reconnaissance Jeeps to give at least some protection to their crews. Flat steel plates in place of the windscreen and side panels on either side served as protection for both driver and front seat passenger. Anyone in the back was left exposed. Another small plate was fitted at an angle from the front bumper to guard the vulnerable radiator in what was otherwise an essentially unarmoured utility vehicle.

There had been a call from combat units for an armoured version and indeed there were efforts to develop one for them. Trials were held with an armour package from the Smart Engineering Company, but it was deemed that the weight adversely affected handling and there were maintenance issues so it didn't proceed. The project was resurrected in 1942 and four different variations were tried, the T25, T25E1, T25E2 and

A Dragon models 1/35 kit of an armoured Jeep, with a .50cal Browning and armour plates in etch brass.

A real Jeep, restored as an armoured Jeep, also fitted with a wire cutter on the front bumper, pictured at Tankfest 2018 at the Tank Museum, Bovington.

T25E3. Again, there was the problem of weight, which badly impacted weight distribution and handling, and reduced the cross-country performance to such a degree that the project was once again halted. For those interested in more detail and archive images, seek out the excellent (but not cheap) reference *Armored Car* by R.P. Hunnicutt from Presidio Press.

In terms of models, there are some Jeep variants available as 1/35 kits from Dragon and, most recently, Meng Models. Dragon has done two versions, one with a .50cal MG and the other with a twin bazooka mounting. The basic kit is a standard Jeep but with etch-brass parts for the extra armour plates. Those etch parts are quite large, flat plates so easier than many etch upgrade sets, which often include some very tiny parts that many modellers find too small and fiddly to cope with. Thankfully, this is not the case with the armoured Jeep, where the use of etch brass works perfectly.

M3A1 SCOUT CAR

The main wartime variant of the M3 Scout Car was the M3A1. Built by the White company, this version had a wider body, the rear door was eliminated, the machine gun track rail was lowered to be within the bodywork and the interior arrangement was changed. It also had the addition of a spring-mounted roller fitted to the front of the vehicle to assist with cross-country performance. With very few changes it remained in production until 1944, by which time 20,894 had been built. They served in all areas of the war and included 6,987 that were supplied to the UK, 3,310 to the

USSR and 104 to China. They were commonly seen with three machine guns – a .50cal plus two .30cal weapons, and these were sometimes the distinctive water-cooled version.

There have been a number of kits of the White Scout Car over the years, the most recent of which is from Tamiya in 1/35 and includes Russian uniformed figures for a Lend-Lease version.

On top of that, there was an old kit by Max, a range that was later released under the Airfix label, and later still Italeri. Despite its age, it is/was actually a rather good kit. HobbyBoss also has a kit in 1/35. There are several kits in smaller scales, one of the earliest being a 1/72 from ESCI, now Italeri, which I think is another really good model for its time. There have been further small-scale models in both resin and metal, while, more recently, a new injection-moulded kit from AccsGB has had some very good reviews, though I have not yet tried it myself.

A White M3A1 Scout Car seen at the War and Peace show at Beltring, Kent, in 2008.

The old Max/Airfix kit of the M3A1 that I built many years ago.

Detailing on the M3A1 Scout Car

The privately owned M3A1 seen at the War and Peace show at Beltring in 2008 provided an ideal opportunity to pick up some super references for getting details right. Here you can see the driver/passenger seats, the interior of the rear body – all painted in the same colour as the exterior – detail of the rail-fitted machine gun mounts, instrument panel, the inside of the two-part door and the back panel with markings but no crew access door.

A White M3A1 Scout Car seen at the War and Peace show at Beltring in 2008.

The car's front seats; the canvas hanging down is the cover for the .50cal Browning machine gun.

Looking back into the crew compartment, note the saw stowed on the inside of the rear plate, and that, as it is an open-top vehicle, the inside is painted the same as the exterior colour.

Detail of the .30cal MG mount on the internal rail.

Instrument panel.

Detail of the interior face of the lower right-hand side crew access door.

Detail of the interior face of the upper right-hand side crew access door, folded down.

The back plate of the M3A1 with the markings clear to see. The ledge above the rear bumper usually carrier the ground tripods for the .50cal and .30cal guns if they were to be demounted from the vehicle.

SIX-WHEEL TYPES

M8 and M20

From a number of different projects and prototypes, the US military selected one six-wheel design that they standardized on, the M8, which came from a Ford design. The prototype T22E2 (with some required alterations to the original T22) was first designed to meet a requirement for a light, mobile Gun Motor Carriage, though this designation was changed to Light Armoured Car when it went into production as the M8. It was only in British service, where it was known as the Greyhound.

A 6x6 design, the early production versions had a small rack for anti-tank mines on both sides, between the front and rear wheel mudguards. Later on this was deleted and the space used for additional, slightly larger, stowage boxes. The turret mounted a 37mm M6 main gun, with a .30cal M1919A4 Browning co-axial MG. To help with anti-aircraft defence, an additional MG ring mount was fitted, with a larger .50cal Browning as well. The M8 proved successful in service and 8,523 were built during its production run from 1943 to 1945.

It is worth noting that the designers recognized that the vehicle was only lightly armoured, so they specified that the fuel tank, at the rear of the vehicle, should be self-sealing. One other point worth noting for modellers if you look through a number of archive images, they were often seen with their mudguards removed. This may have been done due to damage or just to save some weight, but it was seen quite often.

Before looking at some models, I think it makes sense to talk about the M20. Combat units asked for both a command car and a personnel/ammunition/cargo carrier version as well. While they were considered separately at first, it was soon realized that just one design could meet both requirements. This resulted in a prototype, the T26, and that evolved to become the M20 in service. It deleted the turret completely and the top of the hull had the sides raised, bench seats fitted inside, and the top of the crew compartment left open other than above the driver's and co-driver's positions. To provide some measure of protection, a raised MG rail was fitted, which carried a mount for the .50cal Browning. Space in the crew compartment allowed for the addition of a second radio for the command version. Between July 1943 and the end of production in 1945, Ford built a total of 3,971 M20s.

After the war many were given to various European armies, and they remained in service for many years longer. As a result, a good number eventually went into private ownership, so it is relatively common to see them at military vehicle rallies such as the War and Peace Revival. I know of at least two owners of an M8 near me, indeed I have on more than one occasion seen one parked in front of a local pub on a Sunday lunchtime. It's nicely restored and kitted out, and if you ask the owners politely, they will allow modellers who are interested to photograph the interiors.

As for models, there are plenty around and in various scales. One of the oldest kits I can think of is a 1/32 model from the US manufacturer Monogram, first released way back in 1976. Since then we have had plenty of others. The Italeri examples of both the M8 and the M20 are good kits and build easily enough, while Tamiya also has a very good 1/35 model in their range. In fact it was recently re-released in a new set, along with some new crew figures and accessories to provide the basics of a diorama in itself. As ever with Tamiya, the fit of parts is first class. It also has the internal detailing for the crew compartment, so this is one where it really helps to have some reference photos of the real thing, which reveal the stencils indicating the correct stowage location points for the various items the vehicles had to carry.

For wargamers, there are 1/56 (28mm) models from Italeri and Rubicon, both good injection-moulded kits. In the smaller scales of 1/76 and 1/72 there are plenty of options. Again, Italeri features with plastic models, while there have also been metal ones from SHQ and MMS, and resin models from Milicast. Even smaller, there is an older model in 1/87 from Minitanks.

M8 Greyhounds

There are a number of privately owned and restored examples of the US 6×6 M8 armoured car to be seen on the military vehicle show circuit. These detail pictures are from a mix of different ones.

This example of the M8 was in the old arena at the Tank Museum in 2005, taking part in a battle re-enactment demonstration.

This M8 is owned by someone who lives near me and he brought it to a local Vintage Day in 2019.

The turret interior, ammunition rack inside the turret wall and the gun breech.

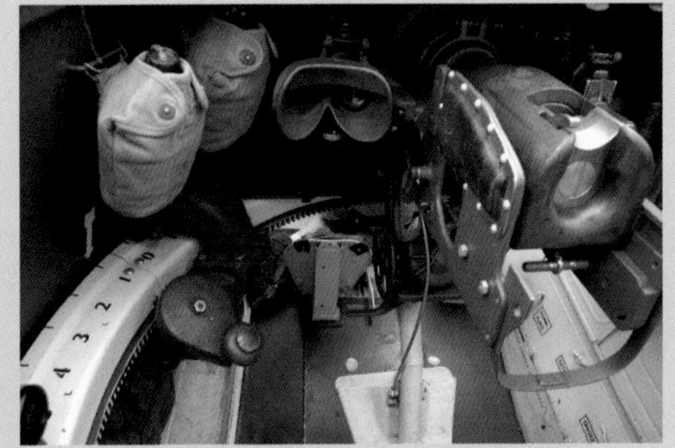

More detail inside the turret, including the head pad for the gunner's periscope, water bottles stowed inside the turret and the numbers on the turret ring to indicate the degrees of traverse applied.

Looking down to see the interior arrangement of the turret.

The instrument panel seen on my local M8.

The driver's position. You can see the interior of this section is painted white inside.

Another example of the M8, this one seen at the War and Peace show in 2012.

Box art for the latest version of Tamiya's M8 armoured car, complete with figures and equipment as the basis for a diorama.

A selection of M8 models, in scales of 1/35, 1/56, 1/72, 1/76 and, smallest of them, the 1/87 Minitanks model.

EXPERIMENTAL TYPES

T17 Deerhound

A requirement from the British Purchasing Commission led to two competing designs for a medium/heavy armoured car. The Chevrolet submission was a four-wheel design that went on to become the production Staghound (*see* Chapter 2), but there was also a Ford design that had six wheels and was powered by two Ford engines. An order was placed for 250 and it was given the name of Deerhound by the British, though none were delivered or used in combat. The ones that were built never left the USA and ended up being issued to police forces with their armaments removed.

There was another six-wheel design, the T19E1, and that had the wheels in a slightly different arrangement with equal spacing between them (rather like the post-war British Saladin series), though again it didn't go into production. It had, however, been given the designation of M38 Wolfhound, a name used for a more modern British army patrol vehicle.

T18 Boarhound

The US automotive industry also experimented with an eight-wheel armoured car, the T18 Boarhound, though like the Marmon-Herrington eight-wheeler, it didn't go into production beyond thirty, eighteen of which were delivered to Britain for testing. It had come from a requirement for a reconnaissance vehicle for use in North Africa, but when that campaign ended, so did the need for what the British referred to as the Boarhound. They were issued in North Africa but only saw very limited service. There is just one survivor, and you can see that in the Tank Museum at Bovington, Dorset.

Thankfully for modellers, there are 1/72 resin kits of both the Deerhound and Boarhound in the Giesbers range, which is available through Black Star Decals in Holland. As for the T19E1, I am not aware of any models out there. As an alternative, there is a great set of scale drawings in the marvellous *Armored Car* book by R.P. Hunnicutt, so could this be a good project for 3D printing?

The T17 Deerhound.

The M38 Wolfhound.

The single surviving T18 Boarhound eight-wheeler on display at the Tank Museum, Bovington.

Rear view of the Boarhound at Bovington.

It's not cheap, but if you can find a copy of Armored Car, *by R.P. Hunnicutt, it is a real gem.*

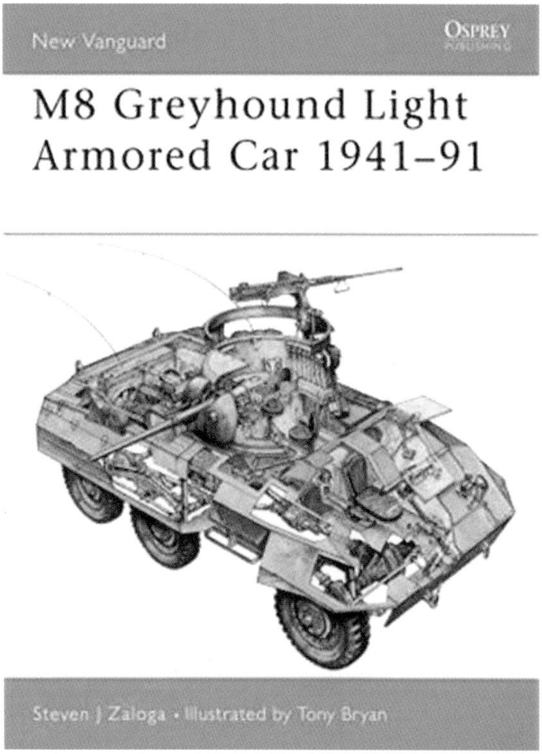

A useful reference on the American M8 armoured car from Osprey Publishing, written by well-known author Steve Zaloga.

Chapter Five

Russian Armoured Cars

FOUR-WHEEL TYPES

BA-20

The BA-20 was a light armoured car built by the GAZ factory, based on the chassis of their GAZ-M1 car, which in turn was based on a Ford chassis. Production started in 1935 and went on through to 1941. They were first used in combat by the Russians at the Battle of Khalkin Gol, in their war against Japan. Others took part in the invasion of Poland and in the Winter War against Finland. A number were captured and one is on display today at the Finnish Armour Museum at Parola. It was used as a scout vehicle and only armed with a 7.62mm DT machine gun, in a small turret. The BA-20 was eventually replaced by the BA-64.

There have been a number of kits on the market over the years. I remember the Alan Hobbies version, though there is a newer one from HobbyBoss that will be better.

BA-64

The BA-64 was a small scout car based on a chassis that was developed by some joint work between Russia and Ford – a small 4×4 chassis that was not only used for the BA-64 armoured car but also the small GAZ-64 utility vehicle, an equivalent to the American Jeep. A key factor about the BA-64 was that the GAZ plant that made them was far behind the front lines, even with the huge advances of the German invaders. While a number of tank factories were famously moved back

A 1/35 scale model BA-20.

out of harm's way, despite the obvious disruption to production, the GAZ factory did not suffer from similar disturbance.

With an angular hull that shows quite clearly an influence from the German armoured car designs such as the Sdkfz 222, it proved to be a successful design. One interesting variant was the conversion for use on railways, the BA-64 ZhD; one version just replaced the tyres with a steel rail wheel, while another had small outriggers at front and rear that could be raised/lowered as required, without needing to remove the standard road wheels. The BA-64B was an improved variant, with a slightly wider chassis, also used in the GAZ-67 Field Car. Overall, it proved to be a reliable armoured car and during the war 9,110 examples of all BA-64 variants were made. It continued to serve after the end of World War II and was used during the later Korean War as well.

For the modeller there is a good variety of BA-64 kits available in 1/72, 1/48 and 1/35 scales. My favourite is the Tamiya 1/48 kit, which builds very easily and looks just right.

BA-64, an Eastern European 1/35 model from a few years ago.

The BA-64, built on the same chassis as the GAZ 64 or 67. This hull design took some influence from the German Sdkfz 222.

The Tamiya 1/48 BA-64, a very neat little kit to build.

A full-size BA-64 seen at the War and Peace show in 2014.

Box art for the recent M3A1 Scout Car from Tamiya, and crew figures in Russian uniforms.

White M3A1 Scout Car

I have already mentioned the American-built White M3A1 Scout Car (*see* Chapter 4), and these were supplied to Russia under the Lend-Lease agreement. They proved to be reliable and popular with Soviet forces and were widely used. For modellers, the latest Tamiya kit comes not just with Russian markings but also with some very nice Russian uniformed crew figures.

SIX-WHEEL TYPES

BA-6 and BA-10

These two armoured cars share the same hull, based on the GAZ AAA truck with a slightly shortened chassis. The base model was a 6×4 vehicle powered by a 4-cylinder 50bhp engine with a four-speed gearbox plus a two-speed auxiliary box. It started life as the BA-3 in 1934, but was quickly upgraded: first into the BA-6, with the same turret as used on the T-26 light tank, then, soon after, into the BA-10, with a smaller, rounded turret. The important difference between both these and the early BA-3 was a notable weight saving. Both were armed with a 45mm gun.

While very much wheeled armoured cars, they are often seen in archive photos either using or carrying a set of tracks that could be fitted around the rear wheels, which would have given them the characteristics of a half-track and better cross-country performance in the snow or mud that were such regular features of the war on the Eastern front where they fought. Production stopped in 1942 but they served on for years after that. One other comment about these is that the spare wheels were not fixed but purposely allowed to freely rotate, which enabled them to aid the car if it was traversing rough ground or ditches.

I am a great fan checking out preserved real-life examples as the ideal reference, and there is a BA-10M in the Finnish Armour Museum at Parola, which is kept in running order. However, it is worth noting that to keep it operational, they have installed a new Ford engine, and this has resulted in the front axle being moved back slightly.

Building a BA-10M

There is a kit of the earlier BA-3 by Zvezda, and both the BA-6 and the BA-10 have been done in 1/35 by Hobby Boss, which are the ones I have tried. For our purposes here, let me talk about their BA-10M.

The build for this one starts with assembling the chassis, which makes it a good example to talk about. Kit manufacturers make different choices with regard to how to break down the parts for construction, and quite a key feature is the chassis, because it needs to be square (level and lined up correctly) for the bodywork to fit correctly and for all the wheels to sit properly on the level. The BA-10 kit is one of those where the main chassis beams are separate parts, and the crossbeams need to be fitted in place to assemble the basic chassis. As you are building it, keep checking that the parts are correctly aligned, and once you are happy with the assembly, leave it on a level surface

HobbyBoss box art for their BA-6 kit.

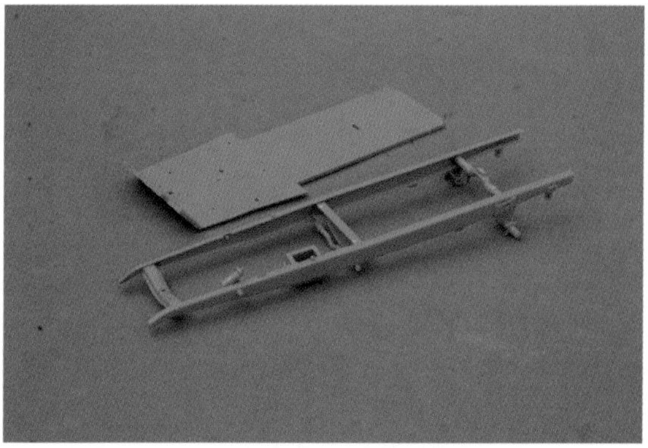

The BA-10 chassis and cabin floor.

Box art for the HobbyBoss BA-10.

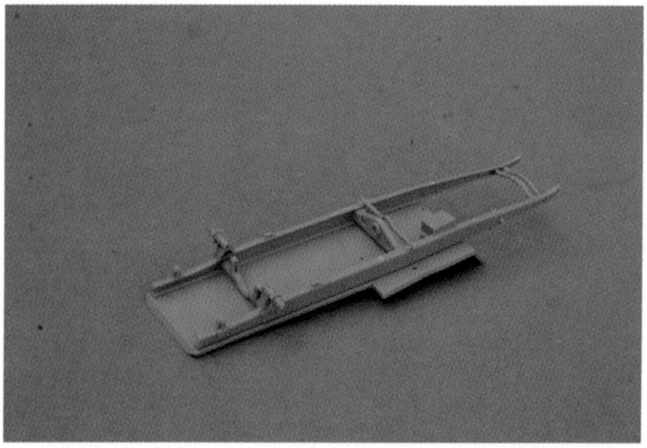

Fitting the floor to the chassis helps ensure you have assembled the chassis to sit squarely within the model.

overnight for the cement to set properly before you add the axles and so on. With this particular kit, there is also a good-size floor for the fighting compartment that can be dry fitted at this point, which helps check that it locates correctly and that the chassis fits flush to it.

With stage 2 in the instruction sequence are the twin rear axles. Do be careful to check you use the correct spring part numbers as there are two lots of Sprue C. I admit I got complacent and made a mistake here, but spotted it in time and was able to sort things out before any cement dried. That aside, the fit of parts is very good. What I didn't do at this point was apply cement to the springs (part 22) yet in fitting them to the axle mountings, which allowed for some movement while fitting the whole assembly in place on the chassis itself.

In step 5 you fit the engine plus two parts that are a bit fiddly – you really need a pair of tweezers to help with fitting the brake linkages, parts S1 and S2. I also suggest doing this when you fit the rear axle assembly and before parts C6 and C7 are fitted in the axle assembly, so they have not dried/set in position before you fit these linkages. This

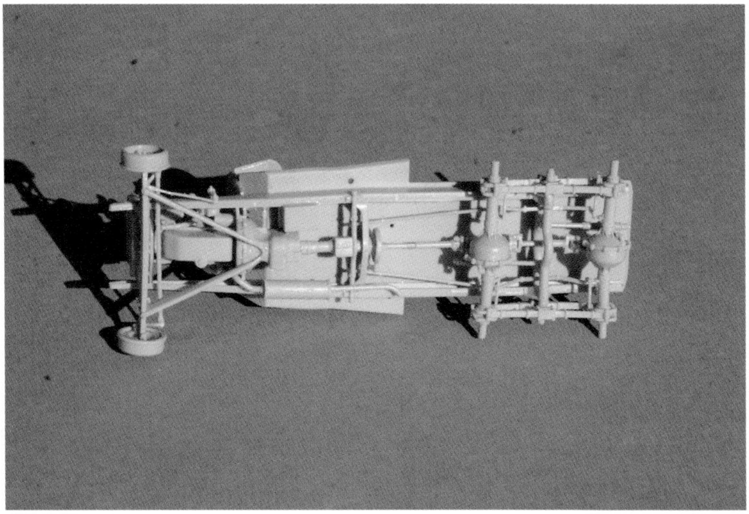

Plenty of detail can be seen in the chassis of the BA-10 while it is under construction.

Chassis, floor, engine and engine firewall all together.

allows you to adjust them that little bit when fitting S1 and S2. This is a well-detailed build but this axle assembly just needs that little bit more care. A benefit of this is that I think it enables you to better understand the construction of the real thing. It does seem a bit of a shame that most of this lovely detail will be hidden away underneath the vehicle once the whole thing is completed, as will the engine. This also applies to a feature we don't often see in kits – the linkages for the driver's pedals into the side of the gearbox. In most kits the pedals simply fit to the floor, but not so with this one.

When it comes to the interior, there is a choice to make. Inside the hull you have details such as the two crew seats, the steering wheel, foot pedals and instrument panel. I fitted and gave a basic coat of paint to them all. However, I am not a great one for dioramas, so won't be fitting a crew and therefore decided to close up all the doors and hatches. Part of that was due to the turret not having any breech detail on the main gun, so if you leave the hatch open without a crew figure, the turret will look very empty. So, closed it was to be. As a result, all of the interior I painted cannot be seen, but I am happier having done it because I know it is there. Strange I know, but one of the points of making models is to be happy with them for yourself.

The next major stage is to fit the bodywork to the chassis. I found this a little awkward at first but actually it works quite nicely. The instructions illustrate placing the main bodyshell down onto the chassis, yet there is nothing to locate it unless you have fitted part S19 to the lower rear edge. Then this locates neatly across the back edge of the floor plate. The sides remain unconnected to anything at this point, so do make sure you dry fit the parts to check the location before you apply any cement. With that in place, add the lower side panels, parts S16 and S17, and you should find it all starts to fit together.

Everything is tied together when you add (as ever, dry fit first to check everything is correctly positioned) the rear mudguards, part S34 and S35. Now the body and chassis are very securely joined and you can add the remaining detail. The instructions suggest fitting the wheels onto the axles at this stage, but I chose not to do this, instead painting the assembled hull and hubs before fitting them. There are some etch-brass parts that need to be bent/fitted as indicated in the instructions, but nothing too difficult. In particular these include the bracing for the rear mudguards.

I had decided to leave this one in plain green scheme, with no winter whitewash as suggested with the marking options. So the basic finish was

Etch-brass parts for the mudguard supports on the BA-10.

easy, just using a spray can of Russian Green Tank Spray from The Plastic Soldier Company. It dries quickly and simply looks right to my eye. Then I brush painted details such as the exhaust and the on-vehicle tools and picked some markings from the kit. Only when those were on did I apply some simple weathering, using various pigments. You can of course choose to do something more elaborate.

Over the years there has been a good selection of both resin and metal models of the BA-6 and BA-10 from the likes of Milicast; I especially like the 1/72 plastic kits from UM Models.

If you would like to know more about Russian armoured cars, there is a recent title on the subject from Osprey (*Soviet Armoured Cars 1946–45* by Jamie Prenatt), but if you can find it, the best reference I know of on the subject is *Russian Armoured Cars 1930–2000* by James Kinnear (Darlington Productions), which has a wealth of detail and plenty of archive reference photos.

The completed 1/35 BA-10 model.

A smaller 1/72 BA-6 by UM Models.

The best reference I know on Russian armoured cars is this volume by James Kinnear.

Another of the informative and well-illustrated Osprey books, which are also reasonably priced, covering Soviet armoured cars of World War II.

Chapter Six

French and Other Allied Armoured Cars

FRENCH MODELS

Panhard 178

The AMD Panhard 178, the Automitrailleuse de Découverte Panhard modèle 1935, was a four-wheel-drive machine, weighing in at around 8 tons, with a crew of four and armed with an effective 25mm gun plus a 7.5mm Reibel MG. It had two driving positions, one front and centre and another facing backwards in the rear left-hand side, so the car could be driven in either direction as necessary. This was a very handy facility in combat, and common to a number of other reconnaissance armoured cars. Over 700 of the Panhard 178 were built before and during the war.

The turret was quite large, unlike on some other French armoured vehicles, and had room for both a gunner and commander, who had seats in a rudimentary sort of turret basket – a 'modern' design that had some gremlins initially, though these were sorted and it did a good job.

The model even went on after the end of the war, when a revised turret and larger 47mm gun were used in the 178B, which saw service in Indo-China. There is a very nicely presented survivor on display in the Musée des Blindés in Saumur, France. When I visited it was on display in the hall with the door open so you could get a close look inside as well.

By far the best reference I have on the Panhard is a small softback book from Editions du Barbotin, which is one of a series of 'Trackstory' books by Pascal Danjou, now sadly no longer available. It describes the 178 in detail, including the development and service history, along with the units the cars served with and all the variations and turrets they mounted, even the unusual ones. It also has the best collection of archive images of the type that I have seen, plus a section on various unit markings. You will find the details in the bibliography at the back of the book, and if you are lucky you might find a second-hand copy on sale.

ICM do a number of very neat kits of the French Panhard 178 armoured car. There are a few variations on the Panhard in the ICM range of 1/35 models apart from the basic French version – one with crew, one with German markings and another German one fitted with a large frame aerial plus railway wheels (and a short section of rail track to display it on), plus the 178B used post-war in Indochina.

Building ICM's Basic French 178 Model

I've built ICM's basic French version of 1940, without any crew figures but with interior detail. You start with the lower hull and the internal floor, along with the engine. This in itself is interesting for having the fan angled sideways, which is unusual. Externally you see the rear engine deck, whereas internally the engine is only on one side, while the other is the space for the rear-facing driving position.

The two side doors can be fitted open or closed, as can the engine covers. Fitting them open will

Panhard 178 at Saumur

There is an excellent example of a Panhard 178 kept at the Musée des Blindés at Saumur, in the Loire Valley. A good feature of the museum is that there are no ropes to restrict viewing and doors are open so you can photograph the interior. Here we can see the front and rear drivers' positions and up into the turret. Note the basic white colour inside, even if it is a little grubby.

The Panhard 178 on display at the Musée des Blindés at Saumur, France.

Open side access door.

The front driving position.

The main floor of the hull and reinforcement ribs are there but the original main floor is missing. This image also shows how dirty the interior white paint would become in use.

Looking up into the turret and the breech of the 47mm main gun.

The rear driving position steering wheel.

If you can find it, the Trackstory publication is the best little reference book on the French Panhard 178.

Box art for the ICM 1/35 kit of the Panhard 178.

The interior of the Panhard built and painted before the bodywork is fitted.

With the hull built and painted, this model shows the armour protection underneath the car.

With the interior of the Panhard done, the sides are glued in place, ready for the roof sections.

allow you to see the nice internal details, but I chose to fix most of them shut, even though that hides the bulk of that lovely detail. I have found over the years that open doors are too easily knocked off, so I tend to shut things up, but at least have the pleasure of knowing the detail is in there (as is the case with all the engine compartment detail in mine). In this case I did decide to leave the rear side door and driving visor open, as well as the top hatch on the turret. All these allow a bit of light into the interior. As the turret can also be lifted off, you will still be able to see the work put into the interior detailing, including the

The Panhard built but with the wheels left off until the hull and wheel wells are painted.

distinctive drum magazines for the 7.5mm Reibel machine gun.

Having built the hull and turret, the only thing I left off until later were the wheels. I painted the hull first, plus the inside face of the wheels, as they have additional linkages there, making it easier to paint them before fixing them in place.

The hull and turret were given a spray coat of primer, while simply using tissue to block the open hatches and stop it from spoiling the already painted interior. They were then brush painted in an overall green. I used an acrylic French Green from a set of French colours but it looked too dark for my eye once it had dried. So, I chose another green, this time a Lifecolor shade, which looked right to me. The next step was to add the dark-brown disruptive camouflage, which was airbrushed on using an Iwata Hi-Line HP-8H, which can manage some fine lines. I felt happy with these once I'd finished; while I could have brush painted them, I do like the softer edges achieved with the airbrush.

The tyres and details like the exhaust were then brush painted before it was time to apply the transfers/decals. While we're on the subject of tyres, I will quickly explain what paints I use. For more years than I care to mention, I always preferred to do them in simple matt black, and in part because it gave a good contrast to Panzer Grey. Once weathering was applied, it looked right to my eye. However, a few years ago, I decided to try something different. The first colour I settled on was a Black Grey shade in the Vallejo range, which I do still use from time to time, but then I discovered the set of black shades by Lifecolor, with six different variations on the theme. I particularly like 'Dirty Black' and 'Tyre Black', which I now use a lot and give me that bit of variation from one model to another rather than all of them being identical. Again, once weathering is applied later, either by dry brushing and/or applying pigments, you can get effects quite simply, and I like simple. Sometimes I see people describe applying weathering effects that just seem to require too much time and effort, making it that much more difficult to complete your models.

The model painted and the wheels fitted.

Completed build of the ICM Panhard 178.

For the camouflaged Panhard, I used the pale-green weathering powder in the Tamiya set to add some emphasis to the detail.

This rear view of the Panhard shows the tools – a shovel and pickaxe. For these, I used a pale buff, then medium brown veins, brush painted on, for the wooden handles. Once dry they were given a final coat of Tamiya Clear Orange to get a varnished wood effect.

Box art for another option, an ICM Panhard fitted with frame aerial and rail wheels.

The Tamiya kit for the Panhard, which is essentially the ICM kit plus added Tamiya accessories.

A 1/72 resin model of the Panhard, perhaps my favourite, by Al.By models from France, which I have had for many years.

Tamiya also have the Panhard in their range, but this is essentially the ICM model reboxed with the addition of Tamiya accessories plus some new markings.

Going back quite a few years, Al.By models in France did manage something of a first, as while they made their beautiful 1/72 resin models (which are still available as I have seen some on the stand of the Dutch shop Black Lion), they also did a 1/35 injection-moulded plastic kit of the Panhard, which was nicely done though never followed up with any more in the range and is no longer available.

Staying with Al.By for a moment, their 1/72 model of the Panhard was one of their early kits that I had. Cast in polyurethane resin, these are really super models, well detailed and equally well cast. The other thing to note is that the firm also did the post-war variant with the later turret, which was used by French forces in Indo-China in the 1950s.

If you can find them, there were a few 1/72 plastic kits by RPM, who did them with at least four turret options.

Laffly-Vincennes AMD 80

Another French armoured car, the Automitrailleuse Laffly-Vincennes AMD 80 (1934–43), was designed in 1931 and in production by 1934. It added a new body to a Laffly chassis that went back to World War I. A number of those built were sent to North Africa (twenty-seven), where they were used against both Italian and German troops up until 1943, when they took part in the victory rally. Main armament in the turret was just a 13.2mm machine gun. It had a crew of four. As with many armoured cars, it had both front and

Small-scale model of the French Laffly. There is a larger 1/35 kit available from Des Kit as well.

rear driving positions so it could be driven in either direction, though with steering only on the front two wheels, it can't have been easy to drive from that rear position.

There is a very nice 1/35 resin model of the Laffly-Vincennes AMD 80 (1934–43) by Des Kit from France. It is quite a straightforward resin kit build, and the detail and fit of parts is excellent. I also like the way Des present their assembly instructions, which include a useful illustrated parts list, so you can both check and identify the parts as you move through the build.

There has also been a smaller 1/76 scale resin kit, which I've had for some years. I think it came from the old Cromwell Models range, but is no longer available.

POLISH MODELS

WZ-34

Built in Poland in the early 1930s, the WZ-34 was a small armoured car, only weighing a little over 2 tons, and powered by a Polski-FIAT engine. There were two versions, the first with a vertical back plate and the second with a sloping back and the turret moved forward slightly. Some were armed with a Puteaux 37mm gun, but most had a 7.92mm Hotchkiss machine gun. They were also fitted with twin rear wheels to aid with stability. They were organized in subdivisions (*dwyizjon*) of nine vehicles, in three platoons of three cars each. However, they didn't fare well when Germany invaded Poland in September 1939, and most had been lost before the end of the month, with very few surviving for the victors to utilize.

As for kits, there has been one in 1/35 and also a couple in 1/72 from different manufacturers. My favourite of them is the most recent, the First to Fight model, which comes with a dedicated magazine on it as well. For a small-scale kit, the First to Fight model is really easy to build and goes together very nicely, plus you get a choice of main armament fit for the turret. No transfers come with the model but the magazine suggests the Polish multicolour camouflage so it makes for a good-looking little model.

Box for the First to Fight 1/72 kit of the Polish WZ-34 II.

Various kits of the WZ-34, in different scales and materials – plastic, resin and metal – and with optional turret armament of cannon or MG.

SWEDISH AND DUTCH MODELS

Landsverk L180/181/182

Among a number of lesser-known armoured cars is the Landsverk L180/181/182, a 6×4 armoured car built by the Swedish company AB Landsverk in the inter-war years. It was not produced in huge numbers and was used not just by the Swedish army but more by the Netherlands and a few by Denmark, Ireland, Finland and Lithuania. Some of the Dutch cars were later put into service by the Wehrmacht, perhaps unsurprisingly, as the different marks were built on German-made truck chassis from Mercedes-Benz, Daimler-Benz and Büssing-Nag. They proved to be quick and reliable, so gained a good reputation among the operators.

There have been a couple of small-scale models over the years, the most recent I know of coming from Den Bels, who also do the 4×4 Pansarbil M/39 in 1/72. Known as the Lynx, the latter was originally built for the Danish army by AB Landsverk; only three had been delivered by the time war broke out in 1939 and the remainder were confiscated by the Swiss army. It had a crew of six and another design with front and rear driving positions plus the turret armed with a 20mm gun.

Landsverk 6×4 armoured car in 1/76.

BELGIAN MODELS

Ford Marmon-Herrington 91Y

The Belgian army ordered sixty-eight examples of the Ford Marmon-Herrington 91Y in 1938–9 to be used as gun tractors for their 47mm anti-tank guns, within their cavalry divisions. The chassis was Ford, assembled in Antwerp, and fitted with a four-wheel-drive conversion made by Marmon-Herrington, and an armoured body also made near Antwerp. After the Blitzkrieg of 1940, many were taken into service with the Wehrmacht, who also used them as command cars.

There is a 1/72 kit of this one in the range of resin models by RetroKit. It makes for another, more unusual addition to any collection of model armoured cars, particularly of the Blitzkrieg era.

Belgian Marmon-Herrington gun tractor.

Chapter Seven

Taking Your Hobby Further

REAL-WORLD REFERENCES

I hope you have seen in this book that there is a lot of scope for modellers within the topic of World War II armoured cars. Rather than purely talk about the many models, I have tried to give some basic information about the real things as well. My intention is to foster an interest not only in building/collecting models, but in the history of the actual vehicles.

When I was young, I used to build a model in order to then play with it. As time progressed, I moved on to painting them and wanting to make them look like the images on the box art. Looking back now, I know that my early efforts were poor. I didn't really understand or appreciate the differences between gloss and matt paints, and that most things were just green and brown camouflage pattern, or occasionally a desert sand colour.

Over time, I began to want to know not just what colour a particular vehicle was, but where, when and why it was that colour. That led me into not only buying modelling magazines for help with basic modelling skills, but into starting to read the histories and campaigns of World War II and delve into the development/evolution of weapons systems throughout the period of the war, between 1939 and 1945. It took me from a youngster playing with toy soldiers to a fascination with history and a greater depth of knowledge on the development of military vehicles themselves, an interest which has not only lasted me for well over fifty years, but one that will stay with me for the rest of my life.

You might get round to owning your own full-size reference material, such as this (deactivated) Bren Mk I, so you can get the colours just right.

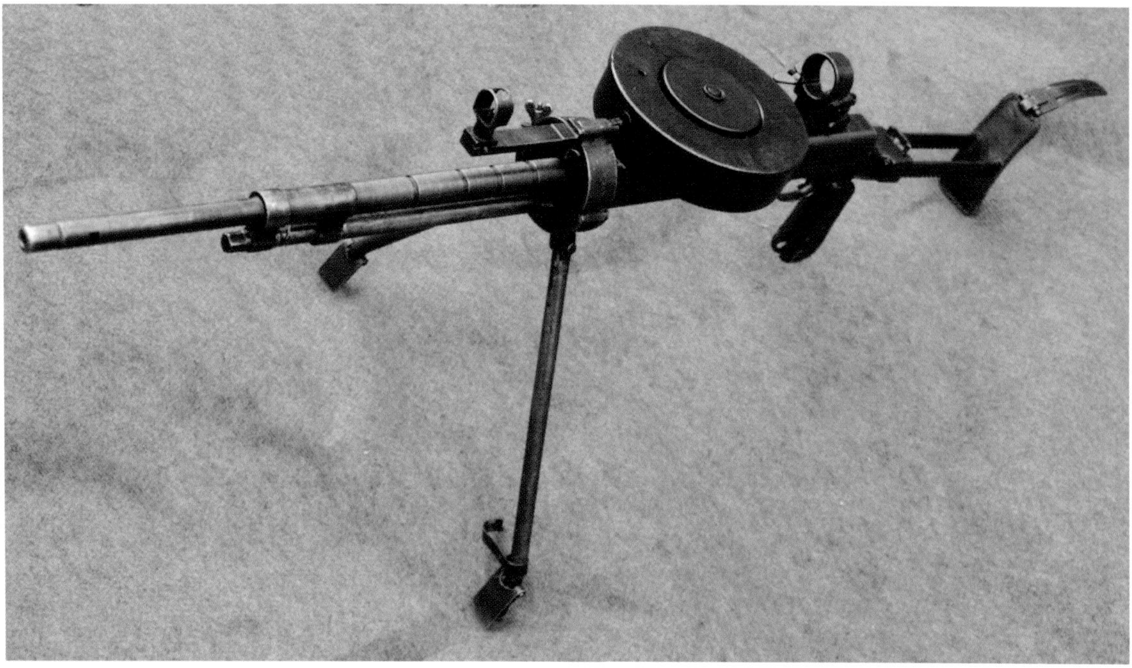

Another AFV-related deactivated gun in my own collection is this Russian DT 7.62mm gun used in many early World War II Soviet AFVs. The bipod could be easily removed/fitted for when the weapon was to be demounted from the vehicle.

One of the paths this can take you down is to take every opportunity to expand your knowledge. This means not just reading books or looking something up on the internet, but visiting local and national model shows, military museums and military vehicle rallies. I for one have never been mechanically minded, so the idea of owning my own has never been practical, though I have given in to buying some real references in the form of some deactivated firearms – much smaller to keep, and the perfect reference for both detail and colours.

At model shows, you will be able to buy new kits and materials to carry on your hobby. I would urge you make the effort to go along to any that you can; attendance at events has been falling over recent years, as so many feel they can get what they need from the internet. The internet is without doubt a very useful tool but it really doesn't replace the friendly atmosphere of a physical event. You can browse trade stands and get the more tactile experience of seeing/touching kits, tools and modelling materials, which you just can't do through a computer screen. Moreover, you have the chance to ask the traders questions about the products they have on sale, many of which are from smaller 'cottage industry' manufacturers that you simply wouldn't have known to look for on the web.

That is not the end of it, though. At an event you can see some beautifully finished models entered into competitions and get lots of inspiration for ideas of your own. You can meet fellow modellers and share your enjoyment of our hobby, chatting with modellers who will usually be more than happy to tell you how they obtained specific effects or just catch up with old friends over a coffee/tea/glass of wine/beer. It is also useful to join modelling organizations such as MAFVA (Miniature Armoured Fighting Vehicle Association) and take advantage of the specialist content of *Tankette* magazine for members. MAFVA is now in its fifty-sixth year of publication.

Now in its fifty-sixth year of publication, Tankette *is the bi-monthly magazine for members of MAFVA (Miniature Armoured Fighting Vehicle Association) and is always a great source of reference information for modellers.*

Other trips out that are very enjoyable are visits to a military vehicle rally/show. Seeing and hearing the real thing is a marvellous experience. Events such as the War and Peace Revival in Kent or the annual Tankfest event at the Tank Museum, Bovington, Dorset have been regular attractions for thousands of people. The chance to see and hear the vehicles in action is good fun, and of course you can take your own photographs for references. Usually the owners of these 'green machines' are very happy to talk to you about them and often allow you to see inside and take more pictures.

Military museums are the other obvious great place to see armoured cars up close. In the UK there are a number of excellent collections. The prime one for armoured cars has to be the Tank Museum at Bovington. Here are examples of a good variety of World War II armoured cars (plus World War I and post-war cars as well), including some experimental ones, such as the eight-wheel Marmon-Herrington Mk VI, the experimental eight-wheeler inspired by the German eight-wheel cars. Seeing them parked close to each other in the display halls, you get a great impression of the disparity in size of the different vehicles. The little Dingo is just that – little, but quick and agile. In contrast, others, such as the Staghound and the AEC, are much larger and better armoured – tough and impressive-looking machines all round. At Tankfest each summer, plenty of armoured cars usually feature in the arena, including the Morris LRC, the Daimler Mk II, Dingo, Marmon-Herrington and of course their iconic Rolls-Royce.

Other museums include the Imperial War Museum (in London and Cambridgeshire), the Muckleburgh Collection in Norfolk and the Cobbaton Combat Collection in Devon, not to mention many smaller,

You might also enjoy checking out military vehicle displays. A rare visitor, seen here in the arena at Tankfest 2017, is a Ford-built Lynx, the Canadian version of the Daimler Dingo.

local museums as well. If you are on your holidays, or simply live outside the UK, there are plenty of other museum collections that are well worth seeing overseas. These include the Musée des Blindés in Saumur, France, the Bastogne Barracks in Belgium, Panzer Museum in Münster, Germany, the Patriotic Park Collection in Moscow, the World War II Museum in Warsaw, Poland and the US Armor & Cavalry Museum at Fort Benning, Georgia in the USA, just to name a few. There are many more, of course, so if you are travelling, always keep your eyes open for promising places that may be close to where you are going.

NEXT STEPS

Another way your interests can be expanded is to consider the history of the armoured car before and after World War II. The motor vehicle with the internal combustion engine was only being developed at the start of the twentieth century, and just fourteen years later the early armoured versions were going to war. They were quite primitive but there was plenty of development in countries such as the UK, France, Germany and Russia throughout World War I.

Post World War II, the picture becomes even more interesting. Through the period of the Cold War and the wide variety of conflicts that have happened since 1945 – including Korea, Vietnam, the Middle East wars, Iran–Iraq war, Indo-Pakistan war, two Gulf wars and of course Afghanistan plus the various smaller and guerrilla conflicts – there have been numerous armoured cars in service with the world's military, partly because they are cheaper to build and operate than more complex tracked vehicles. There have been four-, six- and eight-wheel types, which have also done very well in export sales for a number of countries. Large numbers of the BTR 60, 70 and 80 series have been produced, along with the American-built Stryker and very recently, the European Boxer, a vehicle purchased by the British army in 2020. The excellent World War II German eight-wheelers have clearly been a great influence on post-war designs.

Another way to take your hobby further is to go back to basic model making by finding some scale drawings and using them to scratch-build or make conversions on an existing kit chassis for yourself. There are plenty of sources for scale drawings, but one I would suggest is the MAFVA, as there have been hundreds featured within *Tankette* magazine

If you follow the development of armoured cars after World War II, you will find a whole variety of eight-wheel types used by many countries. This is a US Army Stryker, complete with the added modelling complexity of bar armour, seen at Fort Benning, Georgia in 2013.

This line-up at War and Peace in 2012 shows the various marks of Daimler Ferret, a successor to the wartime Dingo, which served throughout the Cold War and on until the Gulf War of 1991. Many are now in private hands, as those seen here. It was an armoured vehicle with a Rolls-Royce engine and of a size that you could fit in your garage.

over the years. There are also the hundreds that have been drawn over the years by Geoff Lacey, while the large number of plans done by the late Mick Bell are now available to freely download via the internet, at mickbellplans.com. Not all of these are armoured cars and not all World War II, but a lot of excellent material is available.

Some older reference books are still well worth looking out for, on the internet, at model shows or charity shops, where you can often find older books at very reasonable prices.

A much newer avenue to explore for modellers is 3D printing. Rather than having to accurately cut and join plastic card, these day you can transfer

A classic reference, the Historic Military Vehicles Directory *by Bart Vanderveen and After the Battle Publications.*

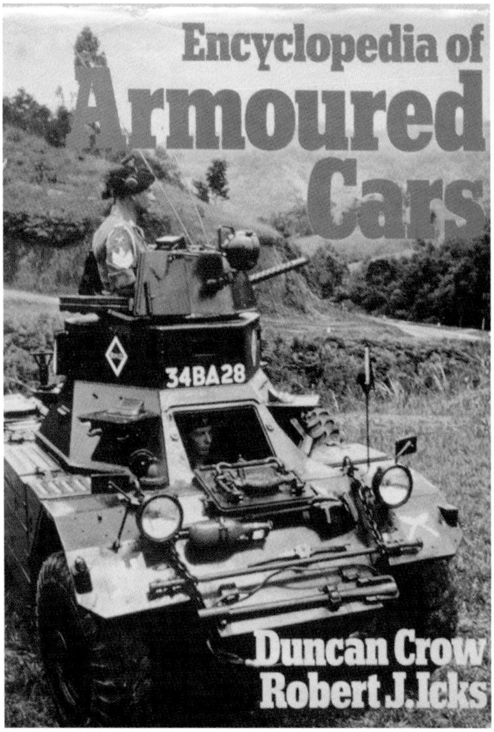

An older reference, if you can find a copy, is the Encyclopaedia of Armoured Cars *by Duncan Crow and Robert Icks.*

Another older reference is A Photo History of Armoured Cars.

the scale plans into a drawing package, create a 3D drawing of what you want and then simply send the file to print. You will have some skills to learn and a choice to make, as there are two quite different types of 3D printer. One uses a reel of plastic filament while the other uses a resin. The resin ones are a bit more expensive and the resin more expensive to buy; it can be a bit more 'messy' but produces the best-quality results. The end result of the plastic ones is not quite as good, as you can see the lines of the filament, but they are perfectly acceptable and of course you can keep printing just as many as you need. It opens new possibilities to encourage newcomers to our hobby and I believe that everything that can do that should be encouraged.

I hope you have enjoyed this ramble around the subject of modelling armoured cars and picked up some ideas of some future modelling projects. Enjoy!

Appendix

The Miniature Armoured Fighting Vehicle Association (MAFVA)

The organization has now been going for fifty-five years, notable for its own bi-monthly magazine, *Tankette*, which is only available to full MAFVA members, and of which I have been the editor since 2017. It is not just a communication tool for the association, but also provides a level of research and reference information that you just don't find in commercial magazines any more. There are also book and kit reviews, keeping members abreast with what is on the market these days, and we encourage members to join in and submit new material for inclusion.

A non-profit organization, MAFVA makes every effort to keep costs down, so at the time of writing, UK membership costs just £18 per year. This modest fee entitles members to a printed copy of *Tankette* six times a year, plus access to even more references and membership benefits via the MAFVA.org website. The cost for overseas membership is slightly more, but only to cover the cost of production and postage around the world. There is an option for membership anywhere in the world for a subscription of just £16.00 per year, but that only gives access to *Tankette* as an electronic copy via the website, not a printed copy. While that is a good way of checking it out, we have found most of those who join on that basis quickly choose to upgrade their membership to receive the paper copies.

The MAFVA website has some content that is freely available but also a separate section that is only accessible to full members. There are some great modellers' references in there plus access to the MAFVA shop, where a number of exclusive and hard-to-find products are available. Local MAFVA clubs that meet around the country offer a great chance for enthusiasts to get together and exchange ideas and generally chat models over a beer or coffee. You will make friends who can last a lifetime.

List of Manufacturers

Company	Material	Scales	Website
Ace Models	Plastic	1/72	www.acemodel.com.ua/en
AFV Club	Plastic	1/35	www.hobbyfan.com.tw/index.php?/&lang=en
Airfix	Plastic	1/76	www.airfix.com
Bronco	Plastic	1/35	www.cn-bronco.com
CA Atkins	Metal	1/72	No longer available
Dan Taylor Modelworks	Plastic	1/72	www.dantaylormodelworks.com
Des Resin	Polyurethane resin	1/35	deskit.online.fr
Dragon Models	Plastic	1/35, 1/72	dragon-models.com
First to Fight	Plastic	1/72	www.facebook.com/firsttofight.p
Giesbers Models/ Den Bels	Polyurethane resin	1/72, 1/76	www.blackliondecals.nl
Gramodels	Polyurethane resin	1/76, 1/150	www.gramodels.co.uk
Hasegawa	Plastic	1/72	www.hasegawa-model.co.jp
HobbyBoss	Plastic	1/35	www.hobbyboss.com/index.php?l=en
IBG	Plastic	1/35, 1/72	www.ibgmodels.com
ICM	Plastic	1/35, 1/72	icm.com.ua
IMA	Resin	1/35	www.imaco.com.hk
Italeri	Plastic	1/35, 1/72	www.italeri.com/en
MAFVA Models	Polyurethane resin	1/72	www.mafva.org
Matador Models	Polyurethane resin	1/76	www.matadormodels.co.uk
MB Models	Plastic	1/72	mbltd.info
Meng Models	Plastic	1/35	www.meng-model.com
Milicast	Polyurethane resin	1/76	www.milicast.com
MiniArt	Plastic	1/35	miniart-models.com
MMS	Metal	1/76	Not currently available

Company	Material	Scales	Website
Plastic Soldier Company	Plastic	1/72, 1/100	www.theplasticsoldiercompany.co.uk
Resicast	Polyurethane resin	1/35	www.resicast.com
RetroKit	Resin	1/72	retrokitonline.net
Reviresco	Metal	1/72	No longer available
Roden	Plastic	1/35 & 1/72	www.roden.eu
RPM	Plastic	1/72	No website
Rubicon	Plastic, polyurethane resin	1/56	rubiconmodels.com
SHQ	Metal	1/76	shqltd.com
Takom	Plastic	1/35 & 1/72	www.takom-world.com/index/product/indexCategory/id/17
Tamiya	Plastic	1/35, 1/48	www.tamiya.com/english/e-home.htm
Trumpeter	Plastic	1/35	www.trumpeter-china.com/index.php?l=en
UM Models	Plastic	1/72	No website
Zvezda	Plastic	1/72, 1/100	en.zvezda.org.ru

Tools/Materials Suppliers

AK Interactive
Paints, weathering materials, tools, books and more
ak-interactive.com

Ammo by Mig Jimenez
Paints, weathering materials, tools, books and more
www.migjimenez.com/en

Deluxe Materials
Filler, superglues, brush cleaner, water effects and more
deluxematerials.co.uk

Evergreen
Plasticard, rod and strip
evergreenscalemodels.com

Humbrol
Paints, brushes, weathering materials, glues and so on
www.humbrol.com/uk-en

Master Tools
Part of Trumpeter organization. Files, jigs, knives, saws, brass tube and lots more
www.trumpeter-china.com/index.php?l=en

Revell
Kits, paints, tools
www.revell.de/en/home

Slaters
Plastikard, rod and strip
slatersplastikard.com

Swann-Morton
Knives, tools
www.swann-morton.com

The Airbrush Company
Iwata airbrushes, Lifecolor paints
airbrushes.com

Vallejo Paints
Paints, weathering materials
acrylicosvallejo.com/en

X-Acto
Knives, tools
www.xacto.com

Bibliography

Cappellano, F. and Battistelli, P.P., *Italian Armoured and Reconnaissance Cars 1911–45* (Osprey Publishing, 2018)

Crow, D. and Icks, R.J., *Encyclopedia of Armoured Cars* (Barrie & Jenkins, 1976)

Culver, B., *Panzer Colours* I, II and III (Squadron/Signal/Arms & Armour Press)

Danjou, P., *Panhard 178*, Trackstory 14 (Editions du Barbotin, 2014)

Forty, G., *A Photo History of Armoured Cars in Two World Wars* (Blandford Press, 1984)

Hunnicutt, R.P., *Armored Car – A History of American Wheeled Combat Vehicles* (Presidio Press, 2002)

Kinnear, J., *Russian Armored Cars 1930–2000* (Darlington Productions, 2000)

Jiminez, Mig, *Illustrated Weathering Guide to WWII Late War German* Vehicles (Ammo of Mig Jiminez, 2020)

Milsom, J. and Chamberlain, P., *German Armoured Cars of World War Two* (Arms & Armour Press, 1974)

Prenatt, J., *Soviet Armoured Cars 1936–45* (Osprey Publishing, 2020)

Ranger, A., *4-Wheeled Armoured Cars in Germany WW2* (MMP Books, 2020)

Scarborough, G., *Airfix Magazine Guide: Modelling Armoured Cars* (PSL, 1977)

Tomczyk, A.M., *Japanese Armor,* Vol. 1 (AJ Press, 2002)

Vanderveen, B., *Historic Military Vehicles Directory* (After the Battle Publications, 1989)

Zaloga, S.J., *Staghound Armored Car 1942–62* (Osprey Publishing, 2009)

Index

RELATED TITLES FROM CROWOOD

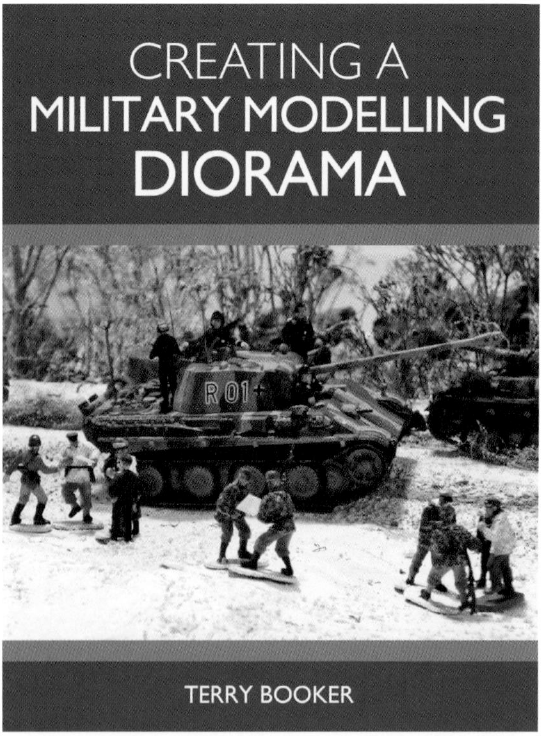

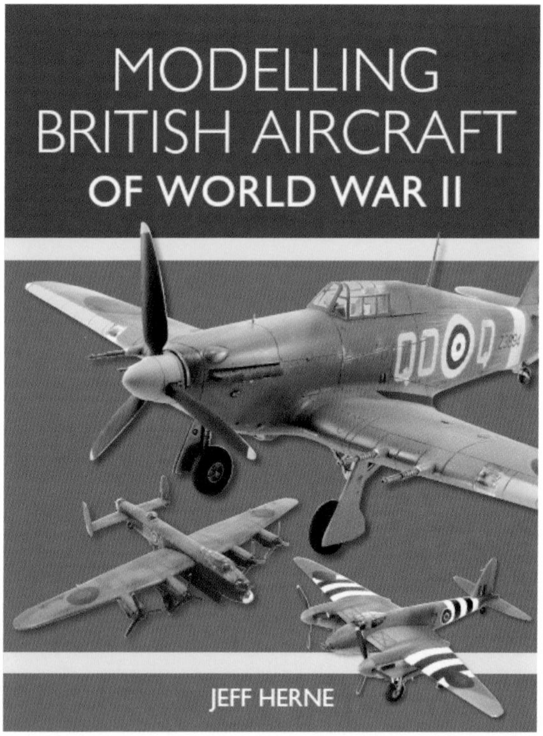

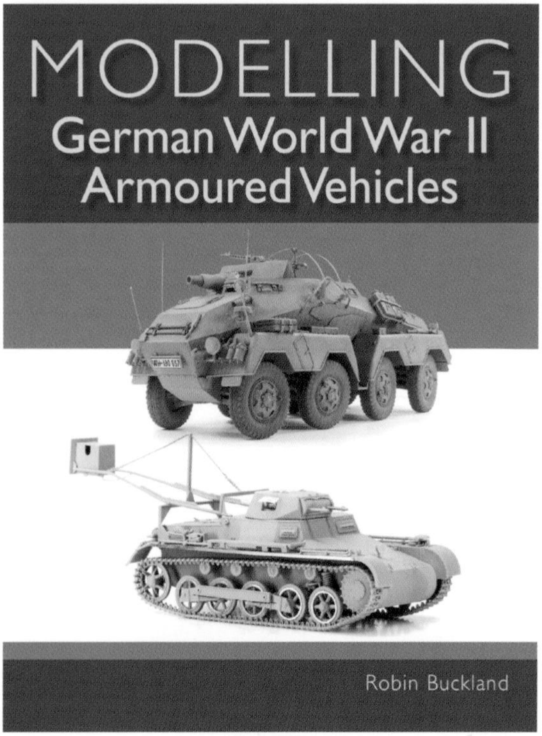